An Introduction to Jungian Coaching

Based on the psychology of Carl Jung, this illuminating new book invites coaches to extend their toolbox with deep, creative, and efficient professional methods that derive from a new perspective on coaching. In using the unconscious archetypes as a practical active psychological database for change, the Jungian coach can contribute significant modification in the coachee's expected behavior. Jungian Coaching can be applied in evaluating the coachee, the team, and the corporation.

This book translates Jungian psychology into simple comprehensive concepts. Each chapter translates theoretical concepts and rationale to the practice of coaching. Illustrated with practical examples from the corporate world and life coaching, it offers Jungian Coaching tools and techniques. By integrating the Gestalt psychology principle of the "here and now" into Jungian concepts, the author develops a new coaching tool that enables an activation of archetypes as a useful and empowering coaching experience.

A valuable introductory resource for all those involved in coaching relationships, this book can empower coachees and serve as a compass for personal growth. It will be of great interest to practicing coaches, executives, human resource managers, consultants, and psychotherapists.

Avi Goren-Bar is a Clinical and Educational Psychologist, Certified Expressive Arts Therapist, Co-Active CTI certified coach, Jungian coach, and member of the European Association of Gestalt Therapy. He is a senior lecturer for the M.A. Art Therapy program at Beit Berl Academic College, Isreal. He is also the manager and senior lecturer in five Expressive Arts Therapy and Coaching programs he initiated in Athens, Zagreb, Ljubljana, Belgrade, and Istanbul, as well as the creator of the Jungian Coaching Method©. Dr. Goren-Bar graduated from the Jerusalem Jungian Seminars program and fulfilled six years of Jungian analysis and supervision. His online International Coaching School and the four Jungian Coaching schools in Ljubljana, Istanbul, Athens, and Budapest are accredited as ACSTH by the International Coaching Federation (ICF).

An Introduction to Jungian Coaching

Avi Goren-Bar

Routledge
Taylor & Francis Group

LONDON AND NEW YORK

First published 2022
by Routledge
2 Park Square, Milton Park, Abingdon, Oxon OX14 4RN

and by Routledge
605 Third Avenue, New York, NY 10158

Routledge is an imprint of the Taylor & Francis Group, an informa business

British Library Cataloguing-in-Publication Data
A catalogue record for this book is available from the British Library

Library of Congress Cataloguing-in-Publication Data
Names: Goren-Bar, Avi, author.
Title: An introduction to Jungian coaching / Avi Goren-Bar.
Description: Abingdon, Oxon ; New York, NY : Routledge, 2022. |
Includes bibliographical references and index.
Identifiers: LCCN 2021020690 (print) | LCCN 2021020691 (ebook) |
ISBN 9780367367985 (hardback) | ISBN 9780367367992 (paperback) |
ISBN 9780429351518 (ebook)
Subjects: LCSH: Personal coaching. | Jungian psychology. | Counseling psychology.
Classification: LCC BF637.P36 G67 2022 (print) | LCC BF637.P36 (ebook)
| DDC 158.3--dc23
LC record available at https://lccn.loc.gov/2021020690
LC ebook record available at https://lccn.loc.gov/2021020691

ISBN: 978-0-367-36798-5 (hbk)
ISBN: 978-0-367-36799-2 (pbk)
ISBN: 978-0-429-35151-8 (ebk)

DOI: 10.4324/9780429351518

Typeset in Times New Roman
by MPS Limited, Dehradun

To Ori, Angie, Tom, Shahar, Maya, Ofir and Dina – my Goren-Bar supporting tribe.
To Ruth Netzer, my mentor and precious compass, to Tine Papic a diamond on the road, to Tanya Zauderer and Dani Golan my assisting team and to my colleagues in the local domestic Jungian Coaching Schools in Ljubljana, Istanbul, Athens and Budapest.

Contents

Epilogue

    Jungian Coaching practice. A personal glance   165

32 When the Shadow archetype met Lady Corona, a
    comprehensive case study about Jungian Coaching in
    Covid-19 pandemic era   167

    Bibliography   180
    Appendix   184
    Index   185

Preface

Professional Coaching is an ongoing professional relationship that helps people produce extraordinary results in their lives, careers, businesses, or organizations. Through the process of coaching, clients deepen their learning, improve their performance, and enhance their quality of life. In each meeting, the client chooses the focus of conversation, while the coach listens and contributes observations and questions. This interaction creates clarity and moves the client into action. Coaching accelerates the client's progress by providing greater focus and awareness of choice. Coaching concentrates on where clients are now and what they are willing to do to get where they want to be in the future.

The basic assumption here is that the potential client functions well on his or her daily lives' challenges, strives to actualize his or her dreams economically, intellectually, and hopefully spiritually as well. People working on a fast-paced innovative environment with rich multicultural teams can benefit from Jungian Coaching, which is a fast, direct, yet very profound, method. Jungian Coaching Method, seems to me, is the laser among all coaching methodologies because it directs the client toward his or her unconscious, focuses on archetypal images that approximate solutions, breakthrough obstacles in efficient techniques, using the coaching sessions as laboratories for change. In this sense, the Jungian Coaching is "Masculine oriented" in the Jungian sense: it is target oriented, structured, and calls for systematic practice based on deep databases. Typically, Jungian analytic therapy is targeted toward prolonged processes of "'Individuation"; however, the Jungian Coaching approach distilled theoretical Jungian concepts and turned them into practical efficient tools for growth, modification, and empowerment.

If you are curious, open-minded, imaginative, fond of symbolism, fascinated by irrational arguments and creativity, yet at the same time you are practical and goal oriented, appreciating intellectual challenges, then Jungian Coaching is the method you may want to acquire.

The Jungian Coaching is based on Carl Gustav Jung's theory. Jung was a Swiss psychiatrist and psychoanalyst who founded analytical psychology. He was born in 1875 and died in 1961 in Küsnacht, Switzerland. Jung's work was influential in the fields of psychiatry, anthropology, archaeology, literature, philosophy, and religious studies. He worked as a research scientist at the famous Burghölzli hospital, under Eugen Bleuler. Depth or Analytical Psychology, which are synonyms to Jungian psychology, encompass tremendous knowledge, which covers, as mentioned, many fields in human sciences. Jungian psychology impacted on understanding the structure of the personality, psychopathologies, psychotherapeutic techniques, spiritualistic ideas, the theoretical rationale for Alcoholics Anonymous, reflections on architecture, opinions about politics, films, and almost anything people are involved with. Jung was a genius, and his followers 'The Post Jungians' added further serious elaborations derived from his writings. It was just a matter of time until the new profession of coaching would land on the shores of this psychological continent.

This book is an attempt to translate into coaching practice what is considered esoteric and "tough to digest" theory. Even more, Jungian psychology is much deeper and vast than what had been sampled to turn into Jungian Coaching. Translating Jungian Psychology into a coaching methodology can be judged eventually upon its applicable capacity. There is one reservation, however, that I feel obligated to state out. Unconscious material, although creative, stimulating and enriching, requires a high level of awareness combined with a strong Ego functioning to be able to contain, elaborate, and actualize. Therefore, it is expected for someone who claims to be a Jungian coach to have experienced and practiced profoundly the method proposed in this book. Because Jungian Coaching generally takes the client gradually yet directly and profoundly into unconscious materials, it requires the coachee to have a strong Ego to be able to face innovative points of views and operative challenges. It requires the coach to acquire Jungian basic knowledge and at the same time be clever, courageous, and search for uncommon observations. One should read this book imagining a coaching safari in a magic jungle.

Theory Part I

Background information

Chapter 1

Introduction on the basics of Jungian psychology

"You live your life fully if you also live what you have never yet lived".
Red Book, Liber Primus (pg. 233)

Jungian Psychology is named after Carl Gustav Jung, a follower of Sigmund Freud. In the heart of Jungian Psychology stands "Jung's unconscious". Both Freud and Jung agreed about the definition of the Id (the primitive and instinctual part of the mind which dwells in the unconscious and contains sexual and aggressive drives). However, Jung differs from Freud's unconscious in that it is considered not solely a hidden "garage" keeping repressed unpleasant contents from early childhood which cause neuroses and other symptoms. Additionally, according to Jung, the unconscious is a psychic domain of libidinal spiritual and highly creative reservoir of potential which, once exposed, empowers a human being with ideas, innovative inventions, authentic behaviors and directs him or her into a developmental quest which Jung called individuation. In Jungian Psychology, what a person does, thinks, senses, and feels are considered the person's "Ego". The "Ego" dwells in the conscious mind and is overt, is witnessed by others, and can be easily stated by the person. However, the unconscious is hidden and is revealed to a person through his or her dreams, art, creativity, drugs, and surprising behavior. Jungian analysis and coaching are aimed at drawing out unconscious materials and applying them into the person's daily life. This process happens through the "transcendent function", which is a psychic instinctual talent which lifts unconscious material to the conscious level. The unconscious, being a creative treasure, contains psychic images that Jung called archetypes. The collection of archetypes functions as an "internal theater" and each archetypal image represents a character (just like the Greek Gods). The relationships between the "functioning ego" (the person) and its unconscious archetypal images (the "Heroes") make our lives exciting and awesome, but yet sometimes frightening. The list of archetypes is long, intriguing, and includes, among many others, the Persona, Shadow, Anima & Animus, Hero, and Trickster. It is advisable to remember that the archetypes are bi-polar (meaning they possess

DOI: 10.4324/9780429351518-1

opposing qualities), and once a person relates to them, their emotional impact is strong. In addition to the two levels of the human psyche (unconsciousness and consciousness) Jung realized a third level, global and collective, which he named: "collective unconscious". With the Collective Unconscious Jung pointed out that humans are born with preliminary psychic innate knowledge about basic life experiences, for example, the instinct of death, motherhood, or cultural traditions. Jung emphasized the importance of dream analysis as he recognized the need to heed, and draw out practical advice, from the deep authentic wisdom of the unconscious. In the last century, Jungian psychology has spread out and impacted different domains of life. In Jungian Coaching, we apply the Jungian knowledge effectively into the coaching practice.

Chapter 2

Active imagination: Activation in the here and now

"I lived into the depths, and the depths began to speak".

Red Book, Liber Primus (pg. 234)

Activation in the here and now stands as the core practice that Jungian Coaching offers the coachee. This technique enables the coachee to activate images, symbols, and archetypes with which he or she will work during the coaching process. This practice increases the coachee's awareness of his or her latent assets. It evokes insights that are essential to coachee's development. The Jungian Coaching method offers a dramatic, highly emotional experience that empowers the coachee. The psychological principles of "Awareness", "Here", and "Now", "Polarities" (experiencing and examining exaggerated behavior toward its extremes) and "Holistic" experience on its three experiential levels (thought, affect, and somatic sensation) are the basis of Gestalt therapy. *Overlapping the Gestalt approach along with the Jungian psychology creates the magic impact of the Jungian Coaching method.* I should comment here that the activation of the archetypes in the coaching session is conceived as a penetrating approach. In Jungian terms we will attribute to such an approach a "Masculine-oriented configuration" (see chapter 19), and such experience requires both trustworthy relationship between the coachee and the coach, skillful coach and strong Ego forces on behalf of the client.

First, let us overview the theoretical background behind the "active imagination" technique. Developed by Jung between 1913 and 1916 (while writing the Red book), "active imagination" is a meditation technique wherein the contents of one's unconscious are translated into images, narrative, or personified as separate entities. It can serve as a bridge between the conscious "ego" and the unconscious and includes working with dreams and the creative self via imagination or fantasy. This approach is meant to ensure that the unconscious contents express themselves *without the overbearing influence from the conscious mind.*

What differentiates coaching from therapy is the autonomy of the coachee to find by himself or herself the authentic resources for solving a problem

DOI: 10.4324/9780429351518-2

and empowering himself or herself to arrive at a decision. "Active imagination" seems an effective coaching method. Von Franz (1964), Jung's preferred disciple, related to Jung's "Active Imagination" and wrote: "Active Imagination is a certain way of meditation imaginatively, by which one may deliberately enter into contact with the unconscious and make a conscious connection with the psychic phenomena. Active Imagination is among the most important of Jung's discoveries" (p. 219). Samuels (1985), a prominent British Jungian analyst and scholar, explains that:

> Active imagination derives from Jung's discovery that the unconscious has an independent symbol-producing capacity. Jung found that this could be used analytically and designated working with such material active imagination to distinguish it from passive fantasizing and also to emphasize that the client may have to make choices based on the outcome of his active imagination. (p. 12)

Later in his book Samuels relates to Weaver (1964), who was practicing Active Imagination, and he commented that:

> the first step in active imagination is that the ego (the coachee) pays attention to psychic fragments and images. The (coachee's) ego can initiate fantasy and be the conscious recorder of such fantasy. Fantasy can be enlarged by participation and intervention of the ego. The more the involvement in the drama the more the ego participates. (p. 202)

Let us deepen the theoretical background that stands behind the Jungian Coaching technique of the "Activation in the here and now". Samuels (1985, p. 81) mentions Zinkin (1979) the Jungian that in his paper "The Collective and the Personal" he refers to Martin Buber's "Principle of Dialogue" as the central distinguishing feature of personal relationships. Martin Buber was an Austrian Jewish and Israeli philosopher best known for his philosophy of dialogue, a form of existentialism centered on the distinction between the I–Thou relationship and the I–It relationship. In his book *I & Thou* (1923) Buber explains that, paradoxically, *if one totally identifies in the here and now with the other (a person or an object), one gets to know him or herself much better.* Based on Goren-Bar (2018, Chapter 4, pp. 161–211, and Goren-Bar 2019, pp. 104–119) and following Zinkin, we choose to activate, in Jungian Coaching, the archetype with which the coachee chooses to practice emotionally, bodily, and mentally. Kast, a leading Jungian analyst, (1992) states that "Jungian psychology offers the techniques necessary to make *the creative potential of the unconscious accessible to consciousness and thereby transform possibility into actuality*".

The Jungian Coaching session prevails in a "coaching triangle space" created between the coach, the client, and the activated symbol in the here and now. By nature, the client brings up in a coaching meeting a dilemma. The coach assists the client in bringing up an image, symbol, or archetype that connects to the dilemma (chapter 3). Stone and Winkelman (1985) strengthen the practical application of Jung's Active Imagination techniques outside the analytic milieu. In their book *Embracing Our Selves: Voice Dialogue Manual* , they state that "Voice Dialogue is really a blending of a number of other systems – Gestalt, Jungian, Transaction Analysis, Psychosynthesis and Psychodrama" (p. 39). They mention three principles for which Voice Dialogue stands for: "(1) Exploration of sub-personalities or energy systems (*meaning in coaching expanding the personality potential*) (2) Clarification of ego (*in coaching, enabling the client to verify and choose between alternatives*), and (3) Embracement of Awareness (*in coaching, increase the client's awareness to as many aspects involved in the dilemma*)" (p. 38).

The Jungian Coaching technique (based on the idea of Active Imagination) is similar to the Voice Dialogue. In the coaching setting, the coachee is invited to locate an empty chair on which a presentation of an image or an archetype or symbol is situated and a dialogue between the coachee and the activated archetype ensues.

The dialogue does not need to be verbal necessarily, but often it turns into an embodiment, dance, sculpture or a dramatic psychodrama.

Figure 2.1 A Coachee - Artifact dialogue in presence of the observing coach. Author's archive.

In Jungian Coaching the coachee practices with Jungian Coaching Cards, games, art, and body work – all aimed at enabling the client to activate the archetypes that were chosen by him or her as empowering assets for their personal growth and change. It will be helpful to quote a few important comments brought up by Stone and Winkelman (1985) to stress the importance of *an aware ego in the coaching process*. "What occurs in active imagination, as in Gestalt work, is that the Ego is often taken over by the Protector/Controller (*as a mechanism of defense*)". This means that at times, the coachee might display resistance to surrender to an irrational dialogue. Such dialogue usually challenges the "decent" logical argumentation that is typical of the client's ordinary language. The more the client is a "thinking oriented" person, the more intuitively he or she will hesitate to try and activate an image. However, by letting go of his or her resistance, the client allows the image an autonomous presence and increases his or her awareness in the coaching milieu. Stone and Winkelman (1985) claim that the client hides behind the Protector/Controller and refuses or rejects the possibility to freely dialogue with the image. He or she usually argues with the coach with rationalizations. They emphasize that "without the Awareness level of an independent outside observer (*I propose here the Coach*), the system is a closed system and the subpersonalities may well remain under the domination of the Protector/Controller. Once an Awareness level is established (*by help of the coach*), and the Ego (*the Coachee*) is clearly differentiated from the Protector/Controller, the method of "Active Imagination" greatly enriches and extends the Dialogue work" (p. 41).

At the place where Stone and Winkelman offer "sub-personalities", Jungian Coaching offers a *reservoir of archetypal images and symbols required to connect to and dialogue with, rendering to interpreting the issues dealt in the coaching process.* Stone and Winkelman see the Voice Dialogue as an "altered state of Consciousness" and "a tangible way of expanding the Awareness level and clearly differentiating it from the other components of consciousness". They explain that:

> After the facilitator (coach) has finished working with whichever voices have been facilitated during a session (archetypes, symbols, images), the subject (the coachee) moves the chair back to the original Ego place and is asked to stand behind the chair. This is the position of the Awareness level. (p. 56)

Chapter 3

Symbolic thought: Seeing beyond the obvious

> "He who possesses the world but not its image, possesses half the world, since his soul is poor and had nothing. The wealth of the soul exists in images".
>
> Red Book, Liber Primus (pg. 232)

The Jungian coach thinks symbolically and encourages the coachee to look at his or her dilemmas through a symbolic approach.

"Coming from the Greek word: *sym* = *meaning together, common, simultaneous, and* the word: *bolon* = *that which has been thrown*, hence, throwing together the things which have something in common" (Samuels, 1985, p. 94). We crucially need to consider Symbolic Thought as the main cognitive-emotional Jungian Coaching way of relating to the coachee and his or her dilemmas. When a client sticks to a concrete dilemma, the Jungian coach wishes to shift him or her into a symbolic understanding of that issue. For this he or she is required to generalize the issue, and for that he or she needs distance from the concrete. When you think symbolically you can dissociate from the concrete actual information, in order to plan and control the action.

In his Collected Works, *On the Nature of the Psyche*, Jung (1954) writes: "The psychological mechanism that transforms energy is the symbol" (p. 45). He adds: "I have called a symbol that converts energy a "libido analogue", by this I mean an idea that I can give equivalent expression to the libido and canalize it into a form different from the original one" (p. 48). This clarification is highly important to the Jungian Coaching practice as this is exactly what we do in our coaching engagement; we hear the client's story and we transform it to the symbolic level. In *Man and His Symbols* (1964), Jung, as editor, not only contributed an article but also recruited his leading team J. Henderson, M.L Von Franz, A. Jaffe, and J. Jacobi, to contribute their knowledge on the psychology of symbols and their significance for comprehending the human psyche. Jung stated that we should learn as much as we can about symbolism; then forget it all when we analyze

DOI: 10.4324/9780429351518-3

our client's dream By stating that once you have learned as much as you can about symbolism, Jung assured that his followers will develop symbolic thinking and, with that, one is not naïve in dealing with images, archetypes, and symbols. McCully (1987) claims that:

> the unconscious speaks through symbols. A symbol emerges as the end product of complex subjective phenomena. We know little about how this takes place. Some aspects of psychic conditions may not conform to the conditions of outer reality. We know this is true in dreams. (p. 21)

Samuels (1985) emphasizes the connection between the Self archetype and the symbol. He stresses Jung's differentiation between symbol and sign, claiming that "the symbolic image 'points to a meaning that is beyond description' as for Jung a symbol is not a sign; that refers to what is already known". Samuels claims that "The psyche spontaneously produces symbols when the intellect is at loss and cannot cope with an inner or outer situation". When Samuels (1985) deals with the theoretical issue "from symbol to image" he tries to clear out the difference between symbol and sign. In relating to Cirlot's (1962) *Dictionary of Symbols*, he quotes the author: "the basic aim of this work is to create a center of general reference for symbolic studies by clarifying the unvarying essential meaning of every symbol" (p. 118). With this theory in mind we should also remember that Kast (1992) the Jungian says: "Creative development becomes visible in symbols and is presented to consciousness by symbols".

Once a spontaneous symbol comes up in the course of a coaching session, how will a client comprehend its meaning? How can we make practical use of this amazing phenomena which the Jungians investigated thoroughly? Why would a Jungian coach need to acquire symbolic thought and how can one work in Jungian Coaching with a symbol?

The trademark of symbolic thought is the language which uses words or images to express concepts (e.g., mother, family). It uses abstract references to transcend concrete reality (e.g., comfort, future) and abstracts to be handled (e.g., mathematical symbols). Symbols are something that someone intends to stand for something other than itself. *Anything can be a symbol for anything else, just so long as someone has intention that that relation holds between those two entities.* Kast (1992) writes: "in order to establish contact to the symbol, we first examine concrete life conditions and then deal with the hidden meaning" (p. 16). In this sense, in Jungian Coaching, it is expected from the coach to analyze profoundly the client's symbol. *The symbol differentiates from its reference by its dual nature.* Real object (picture, map, models) gets a representation of something else which is the "Referent" (something which stands for something else). We should be aware that the symbolic object itself enables lifting it to something else. As Kast (1992) articulates it: "to see beyond the concrete object" (p. 13). We have to learn and investigate with the coachee the picture or image he or she chose in order to know what it represents symbolically. "Generalization" is the challenge here. We have to learn the nature of the symbol and understand the relation between the concrete object/issue/picture and the symbolized image. Representation is a sketching with certain logics, form, and sequence in time and space. "Mother" is a representation. First, she is connected to smell, voice, and contour and then to emotions (warm, cold, love, hate, competition, abandonment). Aniela Jaffe (1964, p. 297), Jung's secretary and Jungian analyst, says something important about the "birth" of the symbol. She claims that the symbol is a common fruit of consciousness and unconsciousness. By this she means that the symbol is created in the intermediate space which is the intermediation between the Matriarch and the Patriarch (for Matriarch/Patriarch read chapters 18 and 19).

Symbolic thought is a human ability to observe a situation, event, relationship, or object (Referent); analyze and comprehend that referent, distant cognitively and emotionally from that specific referent (which has been recently analyzed); and make a generalization so that the specific matter will be granted with *wider significance*. Such significance must encompass the referent yet will take under consideration additional wider references with different meanings beyond what had been perceived in the primer experience of the referent. Stein (1998) reminds us that "surprisingly, there may be a close correspondence between a psychic image and external reality, even when no chance exists that the psyche has been imprinted by it or recorded it from experience" (41). This means that in coaching practice we should take under consideration that the symbol which our client has chosen is very likely connected to his or her actual realistic dilemma.

Jungian Coaching method develops the coachee's symbolic thinking and encourages its preliminary conditions: (1) generalizing, in order to find common factors within the phenomena, (2) imagination and creativity in order to use metaphors, symbols, and images, (3) a high level of emotional intelligence in order to stay away from fixated emotional prejudices, (4) an ability to give up and sustain in order to open oneself up for alternative contexts, and (5) strategic flexibility; analyze the new data obtained from a wider vision expressed in the chosen symbol.

In symbolic thought we should be open-minded to mankind's wisdom, which already possesses most of the human beings' combinations of interests, connectedness, intrigues, and life dilemmas, all of which are coded in human heritage through mythologies, stories, legends, and fairy tales. This immense human psychic repertoire includes most solutions for human conflicts and dilemmas. Symbolic thought can connect a specific dilemma to the accumulated human wisdom. *It is the coach's challenge to connect the coachee to legends, fairy tales, and anecdotes that shed light on the coachee's dilemma.* If our client avoids a generalizing symbolic thought, he or she very likely will fall into the same problems and same failures, avoiding stepping out of automatic habits, of which he or she is accustomed to reacting from. Jolande Jacobi (1964), one of the first Jungian analysts, explains that "the symbol expresses intuitively something which is not explained or expressed by any other way. Following Jung she stresses that we should differ between a symbol and a sign. Signs that have explicit meanings are not symbols. Uniform or the colors of the traffic light are not symbols as they have fixed meaning. Red in traffic lights means "stop!", but red as a color symbolizes emotions. The sign has a casual (reasoning) explanation while the symbol leads toward a purpose: A phallus means a penis yet as a symbol it signifies power, masculinity, control, intrusiveness, fertility, etc. The symbol is bi-polar (like archetype, meaning; has positive and negative aspects) and it is always signifying at something bigger than itself" (p. 383).

We could include that symbolic thought is the client's ability: (1) To observe a situation, event, relationship, or object (Referent); (2) To analyze and comprehend that referent; (3) To distant cognitively and emotionally from that specific referent which has been recently analyzed; and (4) To generalize so that the specific matter will be granted wider significance. Such significance must encompass the referent yet will take under consideration additional wider references with different meanings beyond what had been perceived in the primer experience of the referent.

Symbolic thought is a mode of thinking which opens up a wider scale of considerations for the original referent, a kind of a referred "family" which grants the referent with "sisters and brothers" which are connected to the same psychological DNA. *Example: A businessman in coaching complains about his partners who have taken advantage and cheated on him while he was in a vulnerable period in his life. When being asked: "Such experience, what it symbolizes for you?", he answers: "do you know this Latin proverb: Homo homini lupus (A man is a wolf to another man)?". "I definitely know", I answered and asked: "Where else in your life did you meet such wolves?", and he goes: "Since elementary school, in my family and as a child in overnight summer camps". Now the symbol of threatening wolves helps us in generalizing the phenomena and assists us in trying to comprehend this recurrent challenge.*

Why are the symbol, metaphor, and image essential to the process of symbolic thinking? They are characterized by *condensed structure of visual coded data* which can generalize the overall traits the referent and its re-semblances possesses. A knife can symbolize quite a large category of meanings inferred from its physical traits: Cut (for cooking), murder, carve, analyze, conquer, dig, operate in surgery, victory – all condensed in a one image. According to the principle of conversion each meaning may be converted to another meaning.

In coaching processes, the coach must encourage the client to widen his/her point of view toward different aspects of a dilemma. The ability to use a symbol as a key for symbolic thought will cause a change in the client's attitude toward the dilemma.

We apply symbolic thought through the following process: we analyze (with the client) the dilemma, learn its traits (dynamics and structure), create mental distancing in order to imprint the dilemma into a symbol (or image or metaphor). We present the following questions: This symbol (image, magic word) you have chosen, to which direction it leads your original dilemma? What associates with this symbol? In which way the new connection (association, insight) opens for you a new perspective to cope and how this symbol shades new light on your original dilemma.

Chapter 4

Aesthetic distancing: The arts as the unconscious agents

> "But the small, narrow and banal is not nonsense, but one of both of the essences of the Godhead."
>
> Red Book, Liber Primus (pg. 230).

In Jungian Coaching we search for the client's unconscious wisdom. Arthur Robbins (1989) presents in his book *Aesthetic Distancing Psycho Aesthetic Experience* the concept of the "Aesthetic Distancing". This concept approximates us to the contents of the unconscious. I consider the technique of "Aesthetic Distancing" a very significant and useful contribution to the Jungian coach's toolbox. A client refers to coaching with a dilemma or wish for which he or she expects the coach to help find a solution, a piece of advice or helpful rescue (chapter 11). Even if the coaching approach and competencies call for symmetrical collaboration between coachee and coach, usually the preliminary expected insight or help is attributed and projected by the coachee toward the coach. This dependency on the professional help of an expert derives from the old discipline of the Shaman, replaced later by the medical doctor, and extended to consultants. We must admit that a person in physical suffering only partially needs to cooperate with the medical doctor. In most cases, he or she needs to comply and passively consume medicines – relief will arrive soon enough. However, in coaching, we must have full active involvement from the client's side. When we apply the Aesthetic Distancing technique in Jungian Coaching, we can create a different coaching milieu, which grants the client and coach the amazing opportunity to onset significant change. Once the client presents a dilemma, we can offer a paradoxical approach; instead of approaching the dilemma directly, we can "distance" and ask the coachee to create an artifact, which presents the dilemma in an artistic manner.

DOI: 10.4324/9780429351518-4

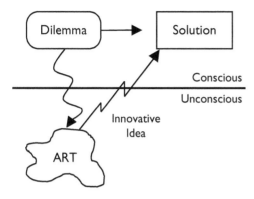

Figure 4.1 The Aesthetic Distancing.

Amazingly, this artistic product, which is created out of inspiration or association with the dilemma, encapsulates a significant hint about the expected solution. Keep in mind that this artistic product, which has been made to present the issue unfolding, does not necessarily need to be beautiful or comply with any artistic or aesthetic standards. It simply needs to display a very idiosyncratic, individual artistic interpretation of the client's issue. The client dives innocently to his unconscious because any artistic process involves unconscious needs, intentions, interests, or considerations. Moving from a verbal report on the dilemma to an artwork designates a gradual shift from conscious to the unconscious level. The coachee tells the coach about his dilemma, the coach suggests him or her to express it artistically, and the art reveals aspects of the dilemma that the client was not aware of. Usually, the artifact exposes the root or bulb that originates the dilemma. Occasionally clients refuse to dive into the unconscious artistically because they are not ready yet. They tend to complain, share their suffering, and express their hope for advice. They need more time, mainly to establish trust with the coach and the Jungian Coaching method. The coach will go on displaying curiosity on the dilemma, ask more questions, and understand better. We proceed by talking about the cause and history of the symptoms involved, until we understand enough. Only after we had discussed the dilemma thoroughly will the client comply to dive into his or her unconscious. When the unconscious is expressed through an artifact, we can try deciphering the artifact, but mostly we should encourage the client to let the art talk. By activating the artistic product, personifying it, and, finally, analyzing it (chapter 2), can we find what added data emerged from the unconscious and how it connects to the client's actual dilemma.

From Jungian psychology to Jungian Coaching

Chapter 5

Jungian Coaching; an economic model

"As a man you are part of mankind, and therefore you have a share in the whole mankind, as if you were the whole of mankind"

Red Book, Liber Primus (pg. 253)

The practical idea behind the *Economic Model,* in Jungian Coaching, is that once the coach acquires the psychological structure and the archetypes of *a single person*, the coach will acquire automatically the psychological and archetypal infrastructure of *a corporation or organization* as well. The assumption here is that they both hold the same psychic structure and contents. Colman (1992), who analyzes "the psyche at work: workplace applications of Jungian analytical psychology", writes that "what holds for the individual's striving for the self, applies even more for the individuating corporation which is striving for the organisational self with its movement towards wholeness and integration of the unconscious" (p. 95).

We can find many evidences in Jungian literature that relate to the parallelism between the particular and the collective psyche (in coaching: the executive and his or her corporation, the person and his or her social environment, etc.). Starting with Jung, who stated that "it's not that we have a psyche but rather the psyche possesses us", and continuing with Neumann (1963), who claimed that there is parallelism between the individual and humanity's consciousness, we get to understand that each individual passes through the course of his or her life the entire process that humanity went through on its consciousness's development. *We learn that there is reciprocity, identical structure, and same archetypal reservoir of contents in both the collective and individual psyche.* Netzer (2004), an Israeli Jungian analyst and author of four books, relates E. Neumann's book on consciousness. She explains that Neumann's idea enables us to consider the individual's developmental processes, as a one element of the entire collective humanity, in which the individual is obviously a natural part (p. 116). We should differ, she stresses out, between *Collective Unconscious and Collective Consciousness.* Accordingly, all social norms, customs and habits, beliefs, and social values

DOI: 10.4324/9780429351518-5

create the Collective Consciousness. In Jungian Coaching we shall refer to the Collective Consciousness of the organization and observe how it is projected on and reflected by the employee's psyche. Neumann (1963) claimed that "the relationship between an individual's problem and collective dilemmas is much more interrelated and tighter than most people assume" (p. 117). Neumann uses the term "Collective Self", claiming it existed much before the emergence of the "Personal Self" because the individual, originally, had been included in the group-tribe that served for him as a Collective Self (as much as the mother functions as the baby's primer Self). Von Franz (1964) explains that the individual's social aspect of the Self, compounds the Collective Social Self. She says that "the Collective Self is bigger than its parts and operates over the individual members of the group". Netzer (2014) further points out to how similar the two processes are: when the "Individual Self" senses that its internal equilibrium is disturbed (meaning when a person is in trauma or stress), it activates a compensatory mechanism. So does the "Group Social Self"; it balances the Collective by creating mutual rituals (e.g., independence days or grief rituals). Edinger (1984), one of Jung's prominent disciples, adds that "the sum of consciousness created by all humans, throughout their entire lives, is cashed in as a constant addition to the archetypal collective human psyche". Netzer (2014) underlines that "from the 20th century on, we can identify an activation and empowerment of the 'Individuation Archetype' which presents the pick of the entire development of humanity. *Some archetypes that operated at the collective psychic infrastructure influenced the Individuation process of all people.* Among those archetypes are (1) the discovery of the secrets of the "depth", (2) the return of the Feminine archetype to the collective consciousness, (3) Death and Resurrection, (4) the Therapeutic archetype, (5) loosening the Patriarch negative side of the super-ego archetype, (6) the archetype of the return of the Repressed, and (7) the archetype of Connectedness and Communication" (p. 132).

Based on this parallel conception between the individual and the collective, *we infer in Jungian Coaching a parallel "archetypal anatomic structure" between the individual and the collective (organization) in the corporate world. We assume parallelism between the "corporate psyche" and the psyche of the individual, executives, or employee.* Therefore, we may postulate in Jungian Coaching that the same psychology that counts for the individual's psychic structure, counts for the team and organization's structure. This means that the same psychology which characterizes Jung's conception of the individual psyche, by token of the collective consciousness and unconsciousness, complies also with the psychology of a group and an organization. We may also conclude that the Jungian coach is qualified to practice on the individual, team, and organizational levels.

We would like to present the Puzzle game picture that summarizes the thesis of parallelism between the individual and organizational psyche. The reader will notice a vertical line. On the left side are the archetypes that we may find in the company, and on the right side the same archetypes as they appear in a person's psyche. You may also identify the three levels of the individual and corporate psyche: the conscious, unconscious, and the collective unconscious levels that are separated by horizontal lines.

Figure 5.1 Puzzle: The Corporate and Individual Archetypes.

The notion that the individual's psychology is as valid as the psychology of the organization or firm, meaning what is true on the micro level is true for the macro level, provides top-quality economizing coaching potential. A team whose individual members have acquired Jungian thinking will also run Jungian-oriented teamwork. They will look for the hidden archetype that blocks them, and search for the appropriate archetype needed to pull them out from an impasse. By the same token, a "management thinking Jung" welcomes managerial policies characterized by using a non-rational agenda and assimilating it on the managerial level of the company.

Chapter 6

Four basic principles in Jungian Coaching

"I have had to recognize that I must submit to what I fear, yes, even more, that I must even love what horrifies me".

Red Book, Liber Primus (pg. 235)

Now we shall present the Psycho-Philosophical principles that comprise the Jungian Coaching infrastructure: (1) The Dialectic Principle and the Unity of Poles, (2) Balancing and the Compensatory Function, (3) Materialism as it relates to Spirituality, and (4) The Transcendent Function.

Enantiodromia (Ancient Greek: ἐνάντιος, romanized: enantios – opposite and δρόμος, dromos – running course) is a principle introduced in the West by psychiatrist Carl Jung. In Psychological Types, Jung (1971) defines enantiodromia as "the emergence of the unconscious opposite in the course of time" (pg. 425). Jung explains that "in the philosophy of Heraclitus, it is used to designatethe play opposites in the course of events - the view that everything that exsists turns unto its opposites" (426). It is similar to the principle of equilibrium in the natural world, in that any extreme is opposed by the system in order to restore balance. When things get to their extreme, they turn into their opposite. Jung adds that "this characteristic phenomenon practically always occurs when an extreme, one-sided tendency dominates conscious life; in time an equally powerful counter-position is built up which first inhibits the conscious performance and subsequently breaks through the conscious control." However, in Jungian terms, a thing psychically transmogrified into its shadow opposite, in the repression of psychic forces that are thereby cathected into something powerful and threatening. This principle was explicitly understood and discussed in the principles of traditional Chinese religion, as in Taoism and yin-yang. A central premise of the I Ching is that yang lines become yin when they have reached their extreme, and vice versa.

If one combines all the above four principles, which correspond to the Enandiodromia notion, one gets the Jungian Coaching practical approach, which is based on paradox, homeostasis, and imagination. In relating to

DOI: 10.4324/9780429351518-6

balancing, compensatory, and the transcendent function, Samuels (1985) states clearly that:

> by taking archetypal theory as a whole, we can see three types of sense-making link: polarity – the positive and negative spectra of the archetype (personal and collective, or instinctual and spiritual), complementary – the relative balance noticeable in psyche; and interaction – the interplay of planes of imagery. (p. 53)

In Jungian Coaching we often lean on the principle of the complementary, meaning the compensatory function. In simplifying this concept, I would state that the opposites are not only opposing each other in life, but, rather, once accepted by the coachee, are compensating as well. This principle is central also in Gestalt therapy. By accepting and adopting this principle practically, the coach can help the coachee to expand his or her repertoire. In teamwork and negotiations, we can mediate through the compensatory function as well.

When Samuels (1985) relates to the *transcendent function,* he explains that "the strength of the person's ego will help the mediatory product or middle position triumph over the two extremes. But the very existence of the mediatory product actually strengthens the ego" (p. 59). Samuels adds that Jung called this process "transcendent function" to emphasize how opposites that could dialogue with each other and engage in mutual influence might actually do so by transcending the old positions in consciousness and unconsciousness and finding a new position, attached to the "ego" (p. 59). Samuels (1985) explains that the *transcendent function* rather:

> mediates between a person and the possibility of change by providing, not an answer, but a choice. This wisdom is, in my opinion, the essence of the coaching ethical codex. He points out that Jung spoke of discrimination (distinguishing ego from non-ego, subject from object, positive from negative and so on) and a capacity to hold the various choices in some sort of balance once they have been discriminated and to facilitate the production of new psychic contents, and hence new conscious attitudes. (p. 59)

Let us summarize those four principles in Jungian Coaching:

1. *The Dialectic Principle and the Unity of Poles* in coaching practice relates to the client's ability to accept contradicting ideas, which should not necessarily threaten oneself but rather open options for a creative collaboration, integration, and synthesis. *This is valid in cases such as "win-win situations" where competing firms coexist in a small market, or when the interest of a profit-oriented corporate engages a philanthropic*

department in their overall business activity, or when divorced parents tend to collaborate on the basis of mutual parental obligations, or when an executive agrees to consider ethical considerations that are against his beliefs for the sake of the company's benefit.

2. *Balancing and Compensatory Function* occurs in coaching processes when the coachee considers inferior situations, non-attractive options, and limited potentials as developmental benefiting challenges. Whatever you lack you might strive to fill up, and what you over possess, you will mistakenly lose. In Jungian Coaching the compensatory function principle is extremely valuable and prevails in most coaching interventions. When a coachee presents a dilemma (obviously reported on the conscious level) and is encouraged by the coach to sort out an unconscious aspect to the dilemma (associate, use arts, use Jungian coaching cards, etc.), often the unconscious contributes *a counterpart paradoxical compensatory point of view* that either empowers the conscious tendency of the client or opposes it. This means that the compensatory function intends to balance the client's inclination; reduce or accelerate the expected. If the coachee presented a dilemma and was asked by the coach to choose an image, come up with a symbol or archetypal image that will represent the dilemma, the chosen image may function as a compensatory symbol (chapter 28). *Example: A mother, in life coaching, came up with a dilemma where she feels her motherhood is characterized by frustration, anger, and stress projected onto her children. She is holding a job in addition to her housewife responsibilities plus her husband doesn't help with the children's obligations. Upon the request of the coach to choose a picture that will relate to her dilemma, she approaches the art buffet and picks from a journal a picture of a male team sailing in a racing boat. This is obviously a Masculine symbol (chapter 19). Why did a Masculine symbol appear from the unconscious to associate with the dilemma? The mother is apparently "Animus possessed"; identifying with a Masculine sport racing team, trying to discipline her children by using too much of the Masculine qualities. By compensatory function, she is advised by her own unconscious to balance her disciplinary approach with Feminine qualities (chapter 18). In this case the unconscious stressed the inflated Masculine repertoire involvement, which is, in the woman's unconscious, found to be exaggerated on account of the Feminine required approach.*

3. *Materialism as it Relates to Spirituality* is discussed in coaching when the coachee or corporation are preoccupied by over-materialistic or financial problems (chapter 25). In such cases ethical or moral issues burst out and require "spiritual balancing". *Example: a nouveau rich businessman overused drugs and alcohol at a roof party and ended up in the hospital. Following that incident, he approached coaching. In the interview it appeared that he reached the top of hedonistic excitement and found no meaning to his life. The coaching dialogue helped him arrive at the conclusion that he must adopt a mindfulness approach to his life.*

The same tenet is acquired when over-spiritualistic point of view takes over the place of realistic and pragmatic steps.

4. *Transcendent Function* is, in fact, another main tool in Jungian Coaching as it is connected to integrating the known with the unknown, in assimilating conscious data.

Later in the book we shall survey the various coaching techniques that enable practicing those psycho-philosophical principles. All those four principles represent a sequence between polarities. The coachee, in presenting a certain dilemma, will locate himself or herself, preconsciously, somewhere in the sequence between those poles. It is the coach's major assignment to enable her or him to not only shift actual experiences and acts along those poles but also to discover the benefits and drawbacks arising by acquiring the life and professional experiences that those sequences offer. Eventually, changing values, behaviors, and approaches are a function of the coachee's flexibility to position himself/herself along those dual poles. However, it is crucial to keep in mind that this "poled structure" is actually the anatomy of our psyche (chapter 14).

Chapter 7

Rosarium – Flipping Principle: A Jungian Coaching way of thought

"If we do not have the depths, how do we have the heights?"
Red Book, Liber Primus (pg. 244)

The Jungian Coaching way of thought is based on a paradox. For me it resembles a classic card game like Hearts, Spades, and Solitaire where the head of the card corresponds to its opposite upside-down twin image. The Flipping Principle is actually a practical version of the compensatory function. It teaches the coach to look at the coachee's dilemma in holistic perception where the coachee's reported arguments are compensated, compared, or balanced by his or her unconscious irrational imaginative internal world.

In his book the *Psychology of the Transference*, Jung (1946), assisted by alchemical pictures, analyzes the relationship between therapist and client. In this complex tissue of relationships (*in our case; coach-coachee*), Jung finds unconsciousness–consciousness reciprocity crucial to the comprehension of the relationship between client and practitioner. He writes:

> It is an unfulfilled program that culminates in the union of opposites. This union is analogous to the "royal marriage" in alchemy. The prodromal events signify the meeting or collision of various opposites and can therefore appropriately be called chaos and blackness. (p. 185)

The collaboration with Wolfgang Pauli (chapter 14) crystalized Jung's understanding of the "Reversal Principle" and its reciprocity, namely, that the unconscious complements consciousness and there is always an "opposing material" standing in compensatory relationship to the "presented actual material". This principle is very practical in Jungian Coaching, and it is displayed in the paradigm of the Wounded Healer archetype. Jung said, "We need another language commensurate with the nature of the psyche" (p. 190). Meaning, this reciprocity between opposing poles is paradoxical and difficult to absorb. Eventually Jung arrived at the "Rosarium Philosophorum", a sixteenth-century

DOI: 10.4324/9780429351518-7

alchemical treatise, with a series of 20 woodcuts that he analyzed. When he investigated the drawing called "King and Queen, Supreme Union of Hostile Opposites" (p. 213), he taught us about the Feminine–Masculine profound relationships, and the depth and importance of the "Flipping Principle", meaning, that there are complementary inevitable compensating relationships between opposites; they do not stand only in reversing positions (as may be seen in first glance), but, from a psychological point of view, they are essential and vital for coexistence. I would like to briefly, in a simplistic manner, analyze the picture following Jung's interpretations, and then point out its relevance to coaching.

Figure 7.1 Rosarium Philosophorum.

Since it is a king standing on the sun (Masculine symbol), and a king is the archetype representing all men, we can infer that the king in the picture is a symbol for the Masculine principle. Same for the queen: she stands on the moon (Feminine symbol) and symbolizes all women, therefore, represents the Feminine principle. The two relate through their left hand, meaning they are in an emotional relationship. Above the two, there is a structure made out of three branches – divinity, and spirituality – bless this relationship through the dove. Jung arrives at the conclusion that we witness in this drawing the *unconscious connectedness* of the Anima (man's Feminine unconscious side, presented by the queen) to the Animus (women's Masculine unconscious side, presented by the king). As a Jungian coach, once you adopt this way of thinking, manifested in the reverse principle of the overt and hidden (which I labeled the Flipping Principle), you can effectively interpret overt and hidden relationships between a corporation and its individuals, between two people in an interaction, between two opposing energies, motivations, intentions, and currents of opposing interests. This "Flipping Principle" adds profoundness and complexity to the understanding of Nature in general and of human beings relationships. A good example will be the phenomena of "manic defenses" where the client describes overloaded daily schedule full with hectic activities (very typical for hi-tech " enslaved" employees) while actually underneath all these activities lies a repressed burnout, waiting for a crises to appear and change the one sided unbalanced equilibrium.

Chapter 8

Individuation: Transcendent function and irrational thinking

"He robbed me of speech and writing for everything that was not his service, namely melting together of sense and nonsense, which produces the supreme meaning".

Red Book, Liber Primus (pg. 229)

Do coachees referring to Jungian Coaching know that they stepped into a possible quest? Do they understand that their Jungian Coaching process has to do with a dialogue they must eventually maintain between what they know (consciousness, what is attributed to the Ego domain) and what they are short of seeing (the unconsciousness, what is attributed to the domain of the Self)? Do they take under consideration that gaining a change or arriving at a crucial decision or expanding personal boundaries all result from what is considered in Jungian psychology as the aspects of the *Individuation Process*?

In the contract between the Jungian coach and the client, there must be, in my opinion, a clearing discussion about the characteristics of this coaching quest. It is finally the coachee's "Self" who will lead the coaching process. The coachee's Ego will dialogue with the coachee's "Self" in order to practically integrate new ideas that are expected to be granted through an Ego–Self axis inquiry. The Jungian coach serves in this contract as a mediator or facilitator ushering the motivated client into the coaching quest.

Here is how *irrational thinking* refers to Jungian psychology and to the way of thinking in Jungian Coaching. Jung discovered the "mystical unconsciousness" by working with hospitalized psychiatric patients (whose hallucinations were visual, powerful, and symbolic) but furthermore through mandala drawings he did between 1913 and 1916 while writing and scratching the *Red Book*. In his famous book *Memories, Dreams, Reflections*, first published in 1963, he mentioned the tremendously powerful meeting with Richard Wilhelm in the early 1920s (p. 405). Wilhelm was a German Sinologist, theologian, and missionary who lived in China for 25 years, became fluent in spoken and written Chinese, and grew to love and admire the Chinese people. When he arrived at Zurich,

DOI: 10.4324/9780429351518-8

Wilhelm validated Jung's discovery of the Self by exposing to Jung his German translation of the Chinese (nowadays well-known) *I Ching* (The Book of Changes). Jung practiced previously the I Ching by producing "practicing sticks" by himself. In the *Red Book* (2009, Pub. Sonu Shamdasani, p. 163), we can see a mandala made by Jung where a golden shrine is surrounded by six protecting walls. Jung found it similar to a Chinese structured image that presented for him the "Self Archetype". In 1963 in the *Memoirs* he wrote:

> What he (Wilhem) told me ... he clarified some of the most difficult problems that the European unconscious had posed to me. On the other hand, what I had to tell him about the results of my investigations of the unconscious caused him no little surprise: for he recognized in them things he had considered to be the exclusive possession of the Chinese philosophical tradition. (406)

The essence of the Chinese and the Eastern approach to the Psyche and Life streams from the *Daoism Philosophy* (I-Ching practice and wisdom sprouts there). This philosophical approach is considered Feminine-oriented in Jungian terms (see chapter 18), and characterized by the *irrational unconsciousness*. The Eastern approach opposes the Western Masculine scientific rationale culture (chapter 19). *Jung found the East as complementary to his previous Western state of mind, meaning uniting the poles.* Jung incorporated in his comprehension of the human psyche both the Eastern and Western philosophical approaches.

The Jungian coach usually offers the coachee tools and techniques that have the capacity to uplift contents from the unconscious. This "elevator" is labeled in Jungian psychology as the "Transcendent Function", and usually the unconscious materials are characterized as irrational, imaginative, humorous, at times rediculous and highly emotional. Kast (1992) argues that "The process of individuation is an ongoing confrontational dialogue between consciousness and the unconscious. The goal of the individuation process is to become who we really are" (p. 1). The coach is challenged to facilitate this dialogue.

N. Schwatz-Salant (1982), a Jungian analyst who investigated on narcissism and individuation, explains that "The ego (the coachee) becomes aware of the fact that its existence partakes of something greater, this awareness requires a capacity for recognizing symbolic reality" (p. 16). That expected change or vision (which the coachee marked as his targeted destination) will finally be achieved through a synthesis between rational considerations (Ego/Coachee's mind), which will be challenged and integrated with irrational options (which derive from the unconscious symbolic reality of the coachee's imagination). Such possible synthesis will finally upgrade or, in Jungian terms, *transcend* the coachee's present Ego repertoire (his/her behaviors, choices, decisions, and acts). In my opinion, the immense process of

Individuation, considered by Jungians as the core purpose of an analytic psychotherapeutic process (which may last a few years), can be humbly considered in Jungian Coaching as a "mini individuation" progression. In the book about Individuation and Narcissism, M. Jacoby (1990) quotes Jung's definition of Individuation: "it is the process by which the individual beings are being formed and differentiated; in particular, it is the development of the psychological individual as being distinct from the general, collective psychology" (p. 94). *We focus here on the essence of the coaching profession that intends to provide clients with the proper conditions to redefine their life or professional needs, targets, individuality, and authentic personal or professional selves.* Jacoby (1990) further adds his explanation as to how the coachee's Ego and Self contribute to his or her development. He says: "what I know of myself is never the totality of who I am. Such terms of 'self-realization' of 'finding oneself' imply that consciousness, with its ego center, strives to discover and experience something of the Self" (p. 50). Samuels (1985), leaning on Jung, claims that this need (*and, if I may add, the coachee's "right"*) of a mature person, to inquire throughout (*coaching process*) one's authentic needs is "a natural tendency". "It is difficult", writes Samuels, "to know who Jung addresses when he talks of individuation. He likens individuation to a drive or sex or hunger, postulating an instinct in man to grow psychologically, similar to ordinary physical maturation" (p. 110). Think for a moment about a potential coachee who calls a coach, and, when the coach asks him or her what made them refer to coaching, they answer: "It's about time I took some steps in my life. I had never dared even utter to myself, I need a coach". Jung states, "Only a man who can consciously assent to the power of the inner voice becomes a personality", but he goes on to say that "the necessary task is to translate the vocation into one's own individual reality" (p. 343). Translating the "vocation into one's own individual reality" happens in Jungian Coaching with the assistance of the coach.

At this point, I suggest shifting for a moment from the "protagonist-coachee" to the "coach" presence in the coaching context. It would be advisable to present to the reader the mythological character or archetype of Hermes-Mercurius (the God of the paradoxical process), whom I see as an inspiring leader for the vigorous practicing Jungian coach who brings forth some irrational thinking into the coachee's repertoire. Netzer (2004) follows Jung (1969) and elaborates on the archetype of Hermes-Mercurius whom Jung described as a Trickster:

A curious combination of typical trickster motifs, can be found in the alchemical figure of Mercurius, his fondness for sly jokes and malicious pranks, his powers as a shape-shifter, his dual nature, half animal, half divine, his exposure to all kinds of tortures and his proximation.

Netzer claims that "in alchemical texts the trickster – Mercury is a vital substance, agent for change, the enzyme of existence, fizz and yeast of body-psyche processes. Mercury is the cause for change, the change itself and the purpose of change" (p. 239). "Mercury", explains Netzer, "by his name symbolizes the fickle, elusive, the misleading, multipolar, the paradoxical and beyond the irrational comprehension" (p. 241). Later she argues: "Mercury is the mediating principle between the various layers of the psyche; Id, Ego and Superego, conscious and unconscious, Ego and Self, between the four functions: Thinking, Feeling, Intuition and Sensation, between Persona and Shadow" (p. 245). "As mediating God, he is a dynamic substance, his freedom is flexibility which is beyond the principle of law or authority. Hermes is the enemy of boundaries; therefore, he passes through them, hence he is innovation and creativity" (p. 246). I claim that an efficient coach is indeed a helpful source agent for change who adopts non-rational thinking and uses symbols and images in the coaching practice. Most coachees, as most people, look for problem solving in domains they are accustomed to, in past solutions, available capacities, or the nearby and familiar environment. Non-rational thinking (as known to us from mythologies) challenges the coachee to dare bring up ideas, wishes, desires, and fantasies in the range of the unbelievable, unexpected, and even forbidden realm. Surely, it is enough that such movement out of the security zone – first in thought only, then by daring to act – will bring the coachee innovative solutions, which will turn him or her into a "Hero" in the Jungian sense.

Practice Part III

Jungian Coaching

Chapter 9

Why practice Jungian Coaching?

"My path is not your path; therefore, I cannot teach you. The way is within us, but not in Gods, nor in teachings, nor in laws. Within us is the way, the truth, and the life.

Red Book, Liber Primus (pg. 231)

Jungian Coaching presents an innovative original approach to Coaching. Coaches, executives, human resource managers, businessmen, leaders, consultants, and psychotherapists can extend their toolbox with deep, creative, and efficient professional methods that derive from a new perspective on coaching. By applying the archetypes of the unconscious into coaching, the Jungian coach can contribute significant modifications to the coachee's expected behavior. Jungian Coaching can be applied to evaluate the coachee, the team, and the organization; it can empower coachees and serve as a compass for personal growth. Jungian Coaching complies with the International Coaching Federation (ICF) competencies.

This method corresponds with D. Kahneman (renowned psychologist and winner of a Nobel Prize in Economics) and A. Tversky's "cognitive biases" (Heukelom 2011), claiming that "humans are not rational creatures yet being irrational is a good thing". As claimed in chapter 1, differing from Freud (who defined the unconscious as a "content repressed" psychic domain that encapsulated unfulfilled desires), C.G. Jung in addition, attributed to unconsciousness a fantastic reservoir of creative potential that strives to be actualized through the "transcendent and compensatory functions" for the purpose of personal "Individuation". The idea of a creative unconsciousness that strives to actualize itself corresponds to contemporary psychoanalysis as presented by C. Bollas's concept of "Genera" (Goren-Bar, 2019).

The uniqueness and added value of Jungian Coaching is that it grants the coachee innovative perspectives on situations, events, and processes at life and work. It enables the coach to see and comprehend invisible contents that activate processes. It provides the employee with concepts that explain behavioral phenomenon and helps develop symbolic thought, as well as an

DOI: 10.4324/9780429351518-9

understanding of unconscious motivations and conflicts. It helps the coachees to attain meaning for their tremendous efforts and investments as well
as their inevitable sufferings, frustrations, blocked states, and inability to
make decisions and tolerate obscure conditions. Jungian Coaching recharges
the system with irrational data that needs to be taken seriously. It fills the
organization's culture with Feminine elements such as expressing feelings,
containment, tolerance, and nurturing; encourages original initiatives,
creative thinking, imagination, and thinking outside the box; and bonds the
individual to the collective, to the past, the present, and the future of one's
own life and business. It investigates the company's heritage, tradition, and
mythology that make solid roots for future vision in corporations.

There have been several attempts to present a Jungian approach to organization in the last few years. Predominant are Corlett and Pearson (2003) with
their pioneer book *Mapping the Organizational Dynamics and Change* that is
practical and bright. Previously, Jones (1996), in *Studying Organizational
Symbolism* , offered comprehension of symbolism in organizations. We can
also find interesting attempts to combine Jungian theoretical glimpses with
case studies that, in my opinion, keep Jungian Coaching merely on a vague
theoretical level. Such examples are Smith (2002) with his attempt to connect
the biblical book of Job to the Feminine principle in leadership. Kociatkiewicz
(2009) uses the concept of Shadow archetype in order to present stories based
on ethnographically inspired field studies of experiencing economic events and
Ketola (2012) with a case study of a female company manager. Some tried to
demonstrate applications of archetypal images to case studies, such as Bala
(2010), showing an interesting interpretation of the Trickster archetype,
Goldberg (2001) using the Hero archetype, and Remington (2007), who uses
biblical mythology to the analysis of leadership. I found Denise's (1997) article
relating to Feminine foundations in organizational psychology impressive.

For a coach to start applying Jungian thinking in his/her training approach, one must learn the basic vocabulary of the Jungian language relating to an individual and to an organization's psyche. It also requires
practicing non-rational thinking by using symbols, metaphors, images, and
archetypes.

It would be advisable to review ten basic assumptions that create the solid
Jungian background theory for corporate and/or individual coaching:

1. The structure of the individual human's psyche applies and is identical
   to the organizational psychology. This means that the entire corporation can be taken as a one human entity for which the Jungian wisdom
   is applicable (chapter 5).
2. Following the model of the Iceberg, any corporation or organization
   operates (from a psychological point of view) like a human being. Imagine
   that 20% of the data dwells on the conscious level and 80% belongs to the
   company's unconscious. The assumption here is that only about 20% of

what is known and familiar to the employee dwells on the overt, reported, and transparent level of communication, while 80% of the data is coded in the unconscious of the organization and its employees.

Example: *The workers in a startup in Israel in which its founders are veterans of an intelligence unit in the army are not necessarily aware of the psychological and ethical norms that prevail in that army unit and were unconsciously adopted by its founders. A recent recruited employee from a foreign country will not possibly be aware of those hidden standards in the firm that are rooted in their army unit. Very likely this "foreign employee" will view these* current *modes of communication and decision making* processes as *incomprehensible* or unacceptable *for him or her.*

3. A corporation is like a vessel. Any organization is a container conceiving a community. In this case it is paradoxically a Feminine organism (womb and fetuses) characterized by Feminine psychology.
4. Every corporation and individual has a Shadow. It is the company's rejected hidden and repressed inferior acts that operate on its employees while they are not aware of its impact.
5. Every corporation has a Psyche. The individual psyche is divided into the personal, the unconscious, and the collective unconscious levels. Accordingly, every company has its "personal story" and its "unconscious history".
6. Femininity has to do with better managerial skills for men. Man's unconscious has a Feminine entity (Anima = relatedness, feelings, creativity, and intuition). Connected with the Anima potential, a manager will relate better to himself and to his colleagues, subordinates, boss, and customers.
7. Women's Masculinity (Animus) has to do with management achievements. Her Animus traits are congruence, targeting, intrusiveness, speed, and logic. Her challenge is to balance her Femininity with her Animus.
8. People tend to confuse Femininity and Masculinity with Sexuality. All men and women have all three traits.
9. Corporations have Heroes. A hero is one who departs from a security zone, exposing oneself to challenges that assist him/her with both ego functions (career) and contact with the Self (spiritual and creative assets). The main assignment of a Hero is to assimilate unconscious drives and ideas to the Ego conscious mind and activities. This role is achieved by balancing opposing forces through mediation between poles into a synthesized personal version of behavior.
10. Every corporation has Tricksters who maneuver in it. The Trickster stage is crucial in the developmental process of the human being or company. It adheres to accelerating processes in the company.

In applying Jungian Coaching on the macro level (corporate life) we should look at the company from a pendulum point of view. We will be moving back and forth; from one pole- executive coaching (which relates to the issue we were asked to coach), toward the opposing pole – the corporate perspective (where the whole company structure, potential, and limitations were previously registered by us on the company's preliminary evaluation). The issue the executive reports about (micro) and the corporate's challenges (macro) are translated first into Jungian concepts, which immediately grant the Jungian coach additional understanding of the issues dealt with. We will usually share our Jungian understanding with our coachees. By doing this, they (executives, teams, managers, or supervisors) will expand their comprehension of the issue unfolding and its hidden meaning. Usually this intellectual, yet creative, process points out at unconscious data that the coachees were not aware of in the beginning of the coaching process. When we *cross the micro archetypal images* (those which relate to the executive) *with the macro archetypal images* (those which correspond to the corporate issues) we learn the contradictions, benefits, and innovative and destructive currents that operate on the individual in the corporation. The insights obtained are like a medical doctor and client waiting for an X-ray on the doctor's computer screen to reveal hidden data about the client's health.

> Example: *From macro perspective: recently, I was asked to lead a team coaching intervention in the geriatric department of a large hospital. The nursing staff was composed of male nurses from mixed backgrounds, Israeli Arabs and Jewish Russian new immigrants. In the hospital hierarchy, both the geriatric department and the male nursing team suffer from low status. The members of the male nursing staff are looked upon as underprivileged employees. I am told that the relationships between staff members are deplorable, creating a shadow over the miserable patients. Jungian analysis of the team brings up several concepts: Persona issues (prejudice about "Arabs" and "Russians"), Archetype of the "Wise Old Man" (a must to transform the Persona of 'old dying patients' into a search for the archetype of the "Wise"; human dignity and wisdom – chapter 27), "Shadow" (the capability of the team to own its inferiority – chapter 21), Connectedness to the "Organizational Libidinal Archetype" and to the "Conjunction Archetype" (discovering the joy of collaboration and the pride of team cohesiveness). From a micro perspective: interviews with men nurses displayed issues such as: personal Shadow; inferiority, law ego functioning, and undeveloped Anima.*

In a feedback meeting with the HR (human resource) manager we agree to schedule eight 2-hour sessions and plan to use creative tools in order to work with the team on Anima, Shadow, Conjunctio (conjunction) archetypes, exposing the team to tasks that will enable them to experience the issues as they unfold. Each experiential activity will be followed by a group process in order to increase the employees' awareness and create change in their attitude toward themselves and their patients.

Chapter 10

Jungian Coaching complies with coaching competencies

"You do not overcome the old teaching through doing less, but through doing more".

Red Book, Liber Primus (pg. 234)

Because Jungian Coaching attempts to apply Jungian concepts to coaching skills, we hereby will compare the ICF required competencies as fitting and complying with Jungian Coaching. The ICF (International Coaching Federation) presents a list of eleven competencies hoping a practicing coach sticks and operates within those professional ethics and skills. Jungian Coaching corresponds and complies with those competencies:

Table 10.1 ICF Competencies Compared to Jungian Coaching

SETTING THE FOUNDATION	JUNGIAN COACHING APPROACH
1. **Meeting Ethical Guidelines and Professional Standards** **Coach clearly communicates the distinctions between coaching, consulting, psychotherapy and other support professions.** **Refers client to another support professional as needed, knowing when this is needed and the available resources.**	Because the Jungian Coaching method puts emphasis on the distinction between therapy and coaching, and because the Jungian theory takes seriously the psychic material of the client, especially his or her unconscious repertoire, and because Jungian Coaching method is built on stimulating the unconscious, we are very much aware of the difference between therapy and coaching. We assure staying in the boundaries of the coaching profession because we strictly are adjacent to the ICF competencies.
2. **Establishing the Coaching Agreement** – Ability to understand what is required **in the specific coaching interaction** and **to come to an agreement** with	Jungian Coaching presents specific tools that enable assessing the client's "Ego Forces" and the client's Latent Potential for growth and change. By offering the

(Continued)

DOI: 10.4324/9780429351518-10

Table 10.1 (Continued)

SETTING THE FOUNDATION	JUNGIAN COACHING APPROACH
the prospective and new client about the **coaching process and relationship.** Understands and effectively discusses with the client the guidelines and **specific parameters of the coaching relationship** (e.g., logistics, fees, scheduling, inclusion of others if appropriate). Reaches agreement about what is appropriate in the relationship and what is not, what is and is not being offered, and about the client's and coach's responsibilities. Determines **whether there is an effective match between his/her coaching method and the needs of the prospective client.**	coach practical specific tools we assure the coaching encounter will be restricted to a mutually agreed coaching plan. In the beginning of a coaching process, it is expected from the coach to explain to the client what Jungian Coaching is about and share his experience from the Jungian Coaching School he or she had attended. As Jungian Coaching creates unique professional vocabulary between coach and coachee, the adoption of this specific coaching language assures that the client is in full awareness to the process he leads throughout the coaching process.

CO-CREATING THE RELATIONSHIP

3. **Establishing Trust and Intimacy with the Client** – Ability to **create a safe, supportive environment** that produces ongoing mutual respect and trust.
    1. Shows **genuine concern** for the client's **welfare and future**.
    2. Continuously demonstrates personal integrity, **honesty, and sincerity**.
    3. Establishes **clear agreements** and keeps promises.
    4. Demonstrates **respect for client's perceptions, learning style, personal being**.
    5. Provides ongoing **support for and champions new behaviors and actions**, including those involving **risk-taking and fear of failure**.
    6. Asks permission to coach client in sensitive, new areas.
	It is highly important to stress out that the Jungian Coaching process prevails in a very structured **"role – triangle"** where the coach (provider), the coachee (leader and consumer), and the Jungian Coaching Tools (stimulants, internal leaders, and internal trainers) are **equal partners.** The coachee sets up a goal for the meeting, the coach helps out provide the right Jungian Coaching tool, and the client starts exploring him or herself on an axis, which, on one pole, presents the dilemma the coachee brought up and, on the other pole, the Jungian Coaching Tool deepens the clients' awareness, behavior, practical practice, and self-given assignments.
	This "teamwork" assures honesty and trust, encourages new learning styles, opens up risk-taking challenges, and obviously discussion about failure and growth.

4. **Coaching Presence** – Ability to be fully conscious and **create spontaneous relationship with the client, employing a style that is open, flexible, and confident.**	Jungian coaches are challenged, during a coaching session, by several assignments at the same time. They obviously need to understand the issue presented by their client as it is unfolding through their "story". They

(Continued)

Table 10.1 (Continued)

SETTING THE FOUNDATION	JUNGIAN COACHING APPROACH
1. Is present and flexible during the coaching process, **dancing in the moment.** 2. Accesses **own intuition and trusts one's inner knowing –** "**goes with the gut.**" 3. Is **open to not knowing and takes risks.** 4. Sees **many ways to work with the client and chooses in the moment what is most effective.** 5. **Uses humor effectively to create lightness and energy.** 6. Confidently shifts perspectives and **experiments with new possibilities for own action.** 7. Demonstrates confidence in **working with strong emotions and can self-manage and not be overpowered or enmeshed by client's emotions.**	must be able to translate the story into Jungian terms, they need to be able to sort out the right Jungian Coaching Tool or technique, they have to know how to present the learning experience to the coachee and discuss whether indeed this is the right technique to experience with; thereafter they must know how to minister the experience procedure (voice dialogue, Active imagination); they have to bring the client to concrete, practical acts or decision and help the client out with homework he or she wishes to register for the next coaching step. All those assignments obviously require the functioning list brought under "Coaching presence". As the Jungian Coaching tools offer simulations, role-plays, artistic productions, body work, using imagination, creativity, and dramatic "here and now" experiences – the holistic experience in Jungian Coaching is one characterized by fun, humor, affect, and surprise alongside string emotional responses such as crying, excitement, and rage that lead to determination. In this sense the Jungian coach must have some Trickster traits too.

EFFECTIVE COMMUNICATION
5. **Active Listening** – Ability to focus completely on what the client is saying and is not saying, to **understand the meaning of what is said in the context of the client's desires, and to support client self-expression.**
   1. **Attends to the client and the client's agenda** and not to the coach's agenda for the client.
   2. **Hears the client's concerns, goals, values, and beliefs** about what is and is not possible.
   3. **Distinguishes between the words, the tone of voice, and the body language.**
	The dilemma that the client brings to the coaching session inspires the coaching content of the session. They practice the Jungian Coaching tools to on the basis of the sketch.
	The experiential Jungian Coaching cards invite the client to experience his or her dilemma on three levels: Mind, Body, and Feeling. This wholistic approach assures high level of body–mind awareness.
	While the client talks to his or her chosen archetypal image, the Jungian Coach listen attentively to the text which comes up spontaneously from the coachee or the image. We encourage the client to repeat three times significant words or

(Continued)

Table 10.1 (Continued)

SETTING THE FOUNDATION	JUNGIAN COACHING APPROACH
4. **Summarizes, paraphrases, reiterates, and mirrors back** what client has said to ensure clarity and understanding. 5. **Encourages, accepts, explores and reinforces the client's expression of feelings, perceptions, concerns, beliefs, suggestions, etc.** 6. Integrates and builds on client's ideas and suggestions. 7. **"Bottom-lines" or understands the essence of the client's communication** and helps the **communication** and helps the client get there rather than engaging in long, descriptive stories. 8. Allows the client to vent or "clear" the situation without judgment or attachment in order to move on to the next steps.	sentences that seem to be incredibly significant to the client's awareness. The idea behind the three repetitions is that in the first repetition the client hears himself, in the second repetition the client understands what he or she meant and in the third repetition the client validates his or her statement (Goren-Bar 2018, Vol.1 chapter 3). The closure in Jungian Coaching is especially important: the client arrives to practical conclusion and builds his or her own homework task.
6. **Powerful Questioning** – Ability to **ask questions that reveal the information needed for maximum benefit to the coaching relationship and the client**. 1. Asks **questions that reflect active listening** and an understanding of the client's perspective. 2. Asks questions that **evoke discovery, insight, commitment or action** (e.g., those that challenge the client's assumptions). 3. **Asks open-ended questions** that create greater clarity, possibility, or new learning. 4. Asks questions that move the client toward what they desire, not questions that ask for the client to justify or look backward.	Powerful questions are common interventions made by the coach on few levels along the Jungian Coaching process. First, during the stage of assessment when the coach needs to help the coachee to focus on a concrete dilemma or framework or target. Second, at the discourse with the "archetypal material" the coach must present questions to both the activated archetype, or image or symbol so that the coachee benefits most from the information given to him by the unconscious; also questions must be presented to the coachee himself or herself in order to be congruent and clear with his desires and purpose of the dialogue. Third, the coach needs to present powerful question especially in the application of the insights aroused by the dialogue with the unconscious. Thus, all in all, the coach is expected to be a vigorous questioning function in the coaching process.

(Continued)

Table 10.1 (Continued)

SETTING THE FOUNDATION	JUNGIAN COACHING APPROACH

7. **Direct Communication** – Ability to communicate effectively during coaching sessions, and to use language that has the greatest positive impact on the client.
  1. Is clear, articulate, and direct in sharing and **providing feedback.**
  2. **Reframes and articulates to help the client understand from another perspective what he/she wants or is uncertain about.**
  3. Clearly **states coaching objectives**, meeting agenda, and purpose of techniques or exercises.
  4. Uses language appropriate and respectful to the client (e.g., non-sexist, non-racist, non- technical, non-jargon).
  5. Uses metaphor and analogy to help to illustrate a point or paint a verbal picture.
	The use of metaphors is common in Jungian Coaching as symbols and metaphors help the client distant from a particular dilemma and generalize a specific argument or problem into a characteristic pattern.
	Reframing and obtaining new perspectives are in the essence of Jungian Coaching as this process resembles the interpretation of a Dream.
	Acquiring the Jungian Coaching vocabulary is essential in the Jungian Coaching as it enables the coachee to conceptualize his coaching quest and deepen his or her awareness.

FACILITATING LEARNING AND RESULTS

8. **Creating Awareness** – Ability to integrate and accurately evaluate multiple sources of information and to make interpretations that help the client to gain awareness and thereby achieve agreed-upon results.
  1. **Goes beyond what is said in assessing client's concerns**, not getting hooked by the client's description.
  2. Invokes **inquiry for greater understanding, awareness,** and clarity.
  3. Identifies for the client his/her underlying concerns; typical and fixed ways of perceiving himself/herself and the world; differences between the facts and the interpretation; and disparities between thoughts, feelings, and action.
  4. Helps clients to **discover for themselves the new thoughts, beliefs, perceptions, emotions, moods, etc. that strengthen**
	The most dramatic and impactful coaching experience in this method is bringing new insights to the client. This happens by increasing his or her awareness. On that crucial, yet amazing, dialogue between the client's conscious mind (what he or she knows, thinks, expects, and brings up in the meeting) to the unconscious (irrational, creative, overwhelming authentic repertoire). This results out of the exciting and stimulating Jungian Coaching tools.
	Jungian Coaching is based on awareness, greater understanding, discovery of underlying concerns, self-discovery in order to practice in the coaching laboratory new repertoires of thoughts, acts, and desires.
	The unconscious will always bequeath the coachee with new possibilities for action to achieve what is important to the client. It is all about seeing different or interrelated factors in an innovative possibility for action.

(Continued)

Table 10.1 (Continued)

SETTING THE FOUNDATION	JUNGIAN COACHING APPROACH
their ability to take action and achieve what is important to them. 5. Communicates broader perspectives to clients and inspires commitment to **shift their viewpoints and find new possibilities for action**. 6. Helps clients to **see the different, interrelated factors that affect them and their behaviors** (e.g., thoughts, emotions, body, and background). 7. **Expresses insights to clients in ways that are useful and meaningful for the client**. 8. **Identifies major strengths vs. major areas for learning and growth, and what is most important to address during coaching**. 9. Asks the client to distinguish between trivial and significant issues, situational vs. recurring behaviors, when detecting a separation between what is being stated and what is being done.	The Jungian Coaching tools provide the Jungian coach with several tool that offer the client ways to estimate his or her major strength vs. major areas for learning and growth. Those areas the coachee is expected to cope with are defined as "inferior functions", meaning the "shadow" of the client. To evaluate the client's benefits and drawbacks the client is required to fill up the "Ego Functioning" Pizza graph. For sampling with which archetypes the client lacks connectedness and requires empowerment Jungian Coaching offers the client to use the Puzzle archetypes and the 24 leadership cards.

9. **Designing Actions – Ability to create with the client opportunities for ongoing learning, during coaching and in work/life situations, and for taking new actions that will most effectively lead to agreed-upon coaching results.**
  1. **Brainstorms and assists the client to define actions** that will enable the client to demonstrate, practice, and deepen new learning.
  2. **Helps the client to focus on** and systematically explore specific concerns and opportunities that are central to agreed-upon coaching goals.
  3. Engages the client to explore **alternative ideas and solutions,**
	The Jungian Coaching tools are based on simulations. The coaching session becomes a laboratory for change. The client defines what he or she needs to upgrade. The Jungian Coaching kit locates the client in within a coaching experience that approximates the client to his or her desired behavior or functioning change. By exploring the unconscious material relevant to the dilemma, the Jungian coach assures an active experimentation and self-discovery on behalf of the coachee; the coach obviously challenges the client's assumptions and perspectives in order to provoke new ideas and new possibilities for action.
	One of the central techniques Jungian Coaching provides the client with are

(Continued)

Table 10.1 (Continued)

SETTING THE FOUNDATION	JUNGIAN COACHING APPROACH

to evaluate options, and to make related decisions.
4. **Promotes where the client applies what has been discussed and learned during sessions immediately afterward in his/her work or life setting.**
5. Celebrates client successes and capabilities for future growth.
6. **Challenges client's assumptions and perspectives to provoke new ideas and find new possibilities for action.**
7. Advocates or brings forward points of view that are aligned with client goals and, without attachment, engages the client to consider them.
8. **Helps the client "Do It Now" during the coaching session, providing immediate support.**
9. Encourages stretches and challenges but also a comfortable pace of learning.
10. **Planning and Goal Setting** – Ability to develop and maintain an effective coaching plan with the client.
   1. Consolidates collected information and establishes a **coaching plan and development goals with the client that address concerns and major areas for learning and development.**
   2. Creates a plan with results that are attainable, measurable, specific, and have target dates.
   3. Makes plan adjustments as warranted by the coaching process and by changes in the situation.
   4. Helps the client identify and access **different resources for learning (e.g., books, other professionals).**
   5. Identifies and targets early successes that are important to the client.
	games that locate the coachee in the center of live simulative experiences. The "Do it now" indeed provides the client with immediate feedback and real innovative experiences.
	
	By connecting to the "Psycho pomp Archetype" (the coachee's internal coach), the coachee learns to commit himself or herself to homework, assignments and practical insights that eventually will cause the significant expected change the coachee's wishes to gain. Jungian Coaching offers the coachee a comprehensive list of references to deepen the understanding the concepts that stand behind their quest.

(Continued)

Table 10.1 (Continued)

SETTING THE FOUNDATION	JUNGIAN COACHING APPROACH

11.**Managing Progress and Accountability** – Ability to hold attention on what is important for the client, and **to leave responsibility with the client to take action**.
  1. **Clearly requests of the client actions that will move the client toward his/her stated goals.**
  2. Demonstrates follow-through by asking the client about those actions that the client committed to during the previous session(s).
  3. **Acknowledges the client for what they have done, not done**, learned, or become aware of since the previous coaching session(s).
  4. Effectively prepares, organizes, and reviews with client information obtained during sessions.
  5. Keeps the client on track between sessions by holding attention on the coaching plan and outcomes, agreed-upon courses of action, and topics for future session(s).
  6. **Focuses on the coaching plan but is also opened to adjusting behaviors and actions based on the coaching process and shifts in direction during sessions.**
  7. **Can move back and forth between the big picture of where the client is heading, setting a context for what is being discussed and where the client wishes to go.**
  8. **Promotes client's self-discipline and holds the client accountable for what they say they are going to do, for the results of an intended action, or for a specific plan with related time frames.**
	The practical assumption in Jungian Coaching is that the exposure and encounter with the leading archetypes will cause gradual change in the coachee's attitudes and behaviors. A follow-up procedure and documented diary of self-reflections are required through the coaching process.
	Shifting back and forth between the "personal" and "archetypal" levels is typical of the Jungian Coaching process.

Table 10.1 (Continued)

SETTING THE FOUNDATION	JUNGIAN COACHING APPROACH
9. Develops the client's ability to make decisions, address key concerns, and develop himself/herself (to get feedback, to determine priorities and set the pace of learning, to reflect on and learn from experiences). 10. Positively confronts the client with the fact that he/she did not take agreed-upon actions.	

Chapter 11

Contract: The archetype of the wounded healer

"If you give up yourself, you live it in others; thereby you become selfish to other, and thus you deceive others".

Red Book, Liber Primus (pg. 249)

Presenting the archetype of the "wounded healer" in the context of Jungian Coaching clarifies the contract between the coach and the coachee. The practical translation of the wounded healer archetype to the coaching milieu lies in the notion that, paradoxically, although the coachee refers to the coach, *it is the coachee who eventually performs the coaching assignment. However, this paradox cannot be accomplished without the active presence of the coach in the equation.*

Greek mythology tells us about Chiron, the Centaurs, half man and half horse. Chiron was entrusted with the rearing and educating of Jason and his sons Medius, Heracles, Aesculapius, and Achilles. Besides his knowledge of musical art, he was skilled in surgery. The Jungians use this mythological story to analyze the therapist–client transference–countertransference re-lationships. We can infer this paradigm to the contract between the coach and the coachee. In the contest between Heracles (the coachee) and the Centaurs (the coach), Chiron (the coach) was accidentally wounded in the knee by an arrow that was poisoned. Grieved at this unhappy event, Heracles ran up, drew out the arrow, and applied to the wound a remedy given by Chiron himself. However, it was in vain; the venom of the Hydra was not to be overcome. Chiron retired to his cave longing to die, but unable to on account of his immortality until, on his expressing his willingness to die for Prometheus, he was released from his misery (based on Stephen Fry's Mythos, 2018).

Let us first understand the complexity of the therapist–client relationship manifested in their contract and how it is dealt with among the Jungians. Then, we shall destilze this know-how into coaching. Samuels (1985), leaning on Meier (1949) and Guggenbuhl-Craig (1971), points out that "the healing practices and rituals in ancient Greece took place within a closed

DOI: 10.4324/9780429351518-11

setting, the temenos or temple" (p. 187). This idea of a safe place restricts the Jungian coach to keep the sessions in a protected location mostly because the tools Jungian Coaching offers require a holding environment. Furthermore, "The analyst (says Guggenbuhl-Craig) becomes the wounded healer in the analytic setting as the temenos permits regression and the giving up of over-consciousness". This means that any therapeutic relationship is calling (from both parties: therapist and client) for regressive interactions. Regressive interactions include, for example, struggling on power or control, need for attention, righteousness, competition, and obedience. Guggenbuhl-Craig (1971) clarifies and stresses that in therapy we talk about an archetype, (meaning that therapy in itself has archetypal qualities). By stating "archetypal qualities" we mean experiences that have *dual opposing characteristics*:

> The image of the wounded healer, with its inherent contradiction, is an archetypal image and, therefore, the bipolarity of the archetype is constellated. But (in therapy unlike in coaching) we tend to split the image so that the therapist figure, in the therapeutic relationship, becomes all powerful; strong, healthy and able. The "patient" remains passive and dependent. (p. 187)

As previously claimed, in the coaching practice this uneven status is prevented.

How does this apply to Jungian Coaching? *Coaching puts emphasis on symmetrical relationships between coach and coachee.* In this sense, the coaching contract eliminates the possibility of a patronizing approach that might occur in a psychoanalytic setting. Coaching competencies refer to an ability to create a safe, supportive environment that produces ongoing mutual respect and trust. Shows genuine concern for the client's welfare and future. Continuously demonstrates personal integrity, honesty and sincerity. Establishes clear agreements and keeps promises. Demonstrates respect for client's perceptions, learning style, personal being. Provides ongoing support for and champions new beings. The coach must ask permission to coach clients in sensitive, new areas, display the ability to be fully conscious and create spontaneous relationships with the client, employing a style that is open, flexible and confident. Coach is present and flexible during the coaching process, dancing in the moment. Has an ability to focus completely on what the client is saying and is not saying, understands the meaning of what is said in the context of the client's desires, and supports the client's self-expression. *Attends to the client and the client's agenda and not to the coach's agenda for the client.* Hears the client's concerns, goals, values and beliefs about what is and is not possible. Encourages, accepts, explores and reinforces the client's expression of feelings, perceptions, concerns, beliefs, suggestions, etc.

If we return now to the coach–coachee relationships in the context of the wounded healer archetype, we can relate to Whan (1987), a Jungian analyst, who speaks in his article about "empathic woundedness" and an "open-wound which indicates inferiority" of the coach. When he develops the concept of "archetypal image of an empathic consciousness" (p. 202), he points out at *an inevitable vulnerability from the coach side, caused by the symmetrical contract dictated by the coaching profession. This contract assures the coach does not take over or patronize the session. The coaching relationships are in accordance with the wounded healer paradigm.* This idea is developed and further presented by Groesbeck the Jungian. In his article Groesbeck (1975), who is interested in the transferential relationships within the Jungian analysis, believes that the therapist "remains forever a patient as well as healer" (pp. 133–134) and he states that "he (the therapist) must also be aware of the dangers of inflations as well as his limitations".

The Jungian coach is vulnerable because finally he remains passive. He can offer the coachee tools to experience, practice, and apply but, nevertheless, he cannot do the job instead of the coachee.

I would like to present Groesbeck's (1975) "Wounded Healer Paradigm" in a simplistic form, which may help the coach accept his limitations, which paradoxically work for the benefit of the coachee.

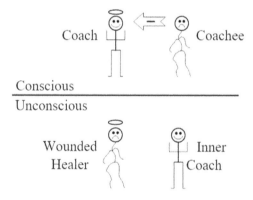

Figure 11.1 The Wounded Healer Paradigm.

The coachee refers to a well-known coach and expresses (on the Conscious level) his concerns (presented in the diagram as minus sign inside the arrow). Active listening and empathic approach, combined by limited ability to act or patronize the coachee (as the contract confines the coach who can only offer the coachee tools to practice with and work out for himself), position the coach, inevitably, in the unconscious domain of the wounded healer. By surrendering to the passive position (of the wounded healer), the coach paradoxically enables and *encourages the coachee to connect to his own internal coaching assets (dwelling in the coachee's unconscious), practice with the tools, and benefit from the empowering experiment.* This process is beautifully summarized by Sedgwick the Jungian (1994, p 26): "The patient *(coachee)* 'illness' must activate the 'personal wounds and/or the wounded -healer archetype within the analyst *(the coach)*. At this point, in order to help the patient *(the coachee)* "the analyst *(coach)* must show himself the way, by experiencing the archetype and its personal ramifications himself. Thus, the analyst *(coach)* is simultaneously a 'guide', a participatory role model and a catalyst for the patient's *(coachee)* 'inner healer'" (Groesbeck, 1975, p. 132).

Chapter 12

Assessment

"I did not know that I am your vessel, empty without you but brimming over with you".

Red Book, Liber Primus (pg. 237)

It is advisable for the first step in Jungian Coaching to evaluate the client's "Ego Forces" (for both individual and corporate coaching). In executive and leadership coaching, as well as in life coaching, we need to guesstimate the clients *personal vs. archetypal* assets. This phase seems vital as it enables the coach to figure out the client's potential for change, ability to face challenges, openness for irrational and imaginative work, and the intensity level of the upcoming coaching process (chapter 8). The conversation between the client and coach on those matters is a preliminary condition to assure the success of the coaching process. Therefore, it is important to present some assessment tools to the client right at the very beginning of the contract. We may offer here the "Pizza" chart, which checks the boundaries of the "Ego Functioning".

In this tool clients are required to fill up 1–10 grades for each invested-spectrum category in their life activities. Obviously, there are potential correlations between the categories, and discrepancies between them can reveal important data that might be relevant for the coaching process. If the total range of activities is generally narrow (small circle), we may assume that the client is limited with his or her Ego assets. In such a case we are expected to go slowly with the client and invest time and efforts to first build up his or her daily performances, in Jungian terms, strengthen the Ego. However, if the "Pizza" is filled up to its edges (big circle), we may assume the person is too active and might have an "Ego inflated" profile. In such a case it is advisable to check what is "swollen" and help the client differentially balance his activity's investment. Any expected change in our lives consumes energy, which inevitably is invested in the account of other activities. Usually the Pizza profile does not display total extremes and the coaching challenge is to analyze together (coach and client) the discrepancies and correlations between the client's overall activities.

DOI: 10.4324/9780429351518-12

EGO FUNCTIONINGS

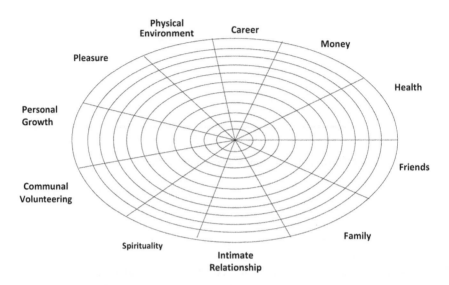

Figure 12.1 Pizza Chart.

Having sampled the coachee-manifested conscious Ego-level functioning (the Pizza), out of a counterpart holistic approach (*which perceives reality as conscious and unconscious oneness entity*), we will evaluate as well how connected the client is to his or her unconscious assets, meaning which archetypes the client is connected to spontaneously. For this indicative part we may use "Archetypal Cards". Taken from the Puzzle game (Figure 5.1), we may offer our client a package of archetypal images and ask him or her to choose three cards. In a Jungian approach we may say paradoxically: "Please check which archetypes (pictures) choose you?" In analyzing the choices the client has made we also face two analytical options; either the client owns the selected archetypal images and identifies with them out of natural proximity, or he or she unconsciously, out of a wishful thinking, is attracted to those archetypal images because they lack what those archetypes represent for them – by a 'compensatory' wish. The same thing counts for a team or corporate diagnostics; evaluate the team or organizational Ego Functioning compared to the team's archetypal images choices (chapter 5).

Example: A housewife who wishes to start a second career comes to a Jungian coach. In an evaluative meeting, on the unconscious level, she selects intuitively three cards: 1) Analysis and Differentiation, 2) Animus and 3) Hero.

1) *The "Analysis differentiation" card, she picked up first, displays a picture of a red umbrella in the center among many other white undifferentiated*

umbrellas. *The text on the back of the card says: The fundamental functions of a "strong ego".It is the ability of human beings to analyze, differentiate, and integrate data and feelings. It relates to all cognitive and affective functions of the conscious mind.*

2) *The "Animus" card, which she picked up second, shows a light pastel hues picture of a young beautiful woman's face in profile. From her shoulder, straight into her head stands a small figure of a young man with a black elegant suit. He stands in affirmative posture facing her with his back to the observer. The text on the back of the card states: It is the Masculine unconscious side in every woman. Once connected to her animus, a woman can develop her ambition, career, intellectuality and physical strength.*

3) *The third picked up card, the Hero, shows the upper part of a knight in an armor uniform, half his face is covered by a shining sword which he holds firmly, while half his face reveals a smile. The text behind the card says: Archetype symbolizing any human quest leaving the security comfort zone and passing obstacles which finally entitle him/her not only achievements but with spiritual understanding of life.*

The combination of those three choices denotes that the housewife is either attracted and highly motivated to a successful career (compensatory function), or that in her actual housewife life she has always been challenging herself into extreme performances. Surely this lady is highly motivated to go on a second career quest and may very likely cope with tough challenges throughout the process. Is that so? We should check her Pizza chart (for conscious level). If her ego functioning is poorly invested, then the archetypal choices display wishful thinking. Yet, if her Pizza chart is well invested on the Ego functioning, and her daily routine is performed efficiently and adequately, then we can lean on her actual potential and support her into a challenging career quest.

Chapter 13

The Jungian Coaching session

"I found you where I least expected you".

Red Book, Liber Primus (pg. 233)

The Jungian Coaching session is a condensed laboratory for change. The target is to penetrate the unconscious to obtain insights, hints, images, and innovative ideas with which the coachee and coach will practice possible options that will satisfy the coachee.

Surely there are sessions dedicated for elaboration and digestion of the insights obtained. In addition, it is crucial to remember that a single unconscious fragment (idea, image, archetype, or symbol) with which the coachee connects to is considered a highly important and significant step in the entire coaching quest. The coaching meeting is held in a triangle structure between the coachee's Ego (manifested by the coachee's argumentations), the coachee's unconscious productions (innovative ideas, creative artifacts, cards experiences), and the coach's assistance. The coach is dedicated to enable a unique evocative experience. The meeting is usually divided into five parts:

Part 1
The coachee presents his/her agenda (narrative, story, argument, or desire, wish or dream). In this part it is important to be congruent and focus on a defined targeted topic. Committed to the coaching competencies (chapter 10), unlike psychotherapy, the Jungian coach is proactive in helping the client move out from complaining, in order to concentrate on the coaching mission of the meeting. *Example: Nathan, a regional manager in an international incorporated multinational manufacturing company, with products sold over many countries, states his frustration and burnout relating to his actual position in the corporation where he had a successful career for many years. He dares to reflect on the idea of quitting his safe job and wishes to think about alternatives but not without very high concerns.*

DOI: 10.4324/9780429351518-13

Part 2

Connecting the aimed topic to an archetype or symbol. In this crucial part of the meeting the Jungian coach is required to associate the topic which was brought up by the coachee to a relevant Jungian concept. Several options are in the inventory of the Jungian coach. *In the above example, it can either be the fifth stage on the Hero Quest; the "Belly of the Whale" (chapter 25). If the dilemma is brought up by the client in a too logical cognitive manner, the coach may assume it would be advisable to connect the coachee to a deeper emotional level that comes along with the dilemma. The coach may offer the coachee to experience the "Anima cards" (chapter 21). However, another option can be an artistic experiment by offering that the client creates a collage (chapter 4), expressing in an artistic manner his frustration, selecting from magazines photos that connect associatively to his dilemma. In the case with Nathan, he chooses to go for that collage.*

Part 3

Next is activating the archetypal image or symbol (which was chosen by the coachee) in the here and now. Here the coach and coachee are expected to dive into irrational voice dialogue experience that is based on the Jungian principle of Active Imagination (chapter 2). This part of the session is the main challenge the coachee is facing. The coaching technique requires an ability to let go of the mechanism of defense, flow into the unknown, trust the coaching process, and lean on the unconscious wisdom (Goren-Bar, 2018, chapter 3). In Jungian terms the coach escorts the coachee to an activated "dream-like" experience, where unconscious choices grant a higher level of awareness that serves as a catalyst for the expected change. *In the example brought up here, Nathan approached an art buffet and selected several magazines. He selected and assembled a collage made out of three photos: Explosion with fire, the Berlin Wall, and a group of alpinists climbing high mountains. The coach asks the coachee "to become" those photos: For the explosion with fire Nathan says: "I am Nathan's nerve system which is about to explode". "I am blocked and suffocated like those in East Berlin before the wall collapsed", he said referring to the picture of the Berlin Wall. Then he paused, looked at the group of alpinists climbing the high mountains, smiled, and said: "I am the long too long way, not without risks, that Nathan will eventually have to go through, in order to set himself free from the corporation after so many years".*

Part 4

The next part of the meeting is dedicated to translate the message or insight into practical behavior or tools to act outside the coaching meeting. At this phase the Jungian coach is expected to assist the client in translating the experience and the unconscious message into practical steps. The crucial point here is not to stay on the known, obvious conclusion (for those are obvious conscious insights that required no Jungian Coaching assistance) but rather explore and interpret the message revealed by the unconscious toward innovative horizons. Questions such as, "where did you go blindly till now?", or "what did this experience teach you"? or "how can you benefit from this experience"? or "how does this experience connect differently to your dilemma?" will lead the coachee into an important insight. *Nathan is stunned. "I was not aware how deep I was in this shit", he says. "It's the mountain track which frightens me the most, and it will be a lonely cruise, I assume".*

Part 5

The closure of the meeting hits toward practice in real life and returning for feedback and evaluation. The ending has to do with a self-contract, where the coachee defines how he or she intends to continue with the insight gained in this coaching session. Often this last part of the meeting considers a possible recruitment of a support group, gaining more information for better decision making, evaluating risks or searching for financial assets. The Ego is now challenged to incorporate the message from the unconscious. *"If this is how you really feel, says the Jungian coach to Nathan, then maybe it is time to seriously consider the planning of your next steps".*

This example displayed only one optional transcendent function technique out of many other optional interventions. The use of a metaphor or symbol grants the coachee a visual-emotional code, such as an icon, to which he or she can connect in the face of challenge or conflict. Memorizing the coaching session and its insights will help adhere to what was agreed, understood, committed, and internalized during the course of the coaching sessions.

Archetypes applied to coaching

Chapter 14

Archetypal and complex coaching: The inner theatre

"Whoever looks from inside, knows that everything is new. The events that happen are always the same. But the creative depths of man are not always the same. We create the meaning of events. The meaning is and always was artificial. We make it".

Red Book, Liber Primus (pg. 239)

Imagine the unconscious of the coachee is a pharmacy, and on its shelves are arranged those psychic energetic amazing potentials, which, once brought up through the transcendent function to the coachee's awareness, can cause a significant change for good or bad on his or her overt behavior. Samuels (1985) relates to the "hierarchy" of the archetypes and puts it in his own words as follows:

Starting from the outside and looking in, is a traditional way to proceed. In this system, we first meet the Persona archetype…continuing inwards, the next discrete archetype is the Shadow … next we consider the contra sexual archetypes, Anima and Animus … the innermost archetype is the Self. (p. 31)

He explains: "Because archetypal layers of the psyche are fundamental, they tend to produce images and situations which have a tremendous impact on the individual, gripping him and holding him in a grip, often, but not always, with an accompanying feeling of mystery, and will be unable to remain unaffected" (p. 29). This statement clarifies the Jungian Coaching approach combining emotional and intellectual materials together. Since archetypal psychic storage is one of Jungian Coaching's main tools, we would like to propose a table displaying the basic practical archetypes we work with both, on the executive/individual coaching level and in corporate and organizational frameworks. If any of our interpretations attributed to the archetypes cause some uneasiness to the reader, I suggest reading in depth the following survey of the theoretical background to overcome certain prejudices. As Jung (1982) wrote himself:

DOI: 10.4324/9780429351518-14

I do not expect every reader to grasp right away what is meant by animus and anima. But I hope he will at least have gained the impression that this is not a question of anything "metaphysical" but far rather of empirical facts which could equally well be expressed in rational and abstract language. (100)

Bolen (1989) prefers to present the archetypes through the cases of the Greek Gods and Goddesses arguing that:

Getting to know the Gods is a source for empowerment ... we shall encounter each of the Gods, shifting from the God image towards mythology and forth to the archetype. We shall see how each of the Gods impacts the personality and its preferences, we shall learn in addition how meanings and psychological challenges are interconnected in the archetypal Gods. (p. 31, Hebrew translation)

Table 14.1 The Individual Archetypes Translated to Corporation World.

Archetype	Individual	Organization
Analysis & Differentiation	Are basic functions of a "strong Ego". It's human ability to analyze, differentiate, and integrate data and feeling. It relates to all cognitive, physical, and affective functions.	Is the organization's ability to scan out its activities and dynamics in order to arrive to conclusions and improve performances.
Anima	Is the Feminine unconscious side in every man, once connected to his anima a man can develop his affect, intuition, creativity, containment, processing, and expressivity.	On macro level it is the value an organization holds to promote, nurture, support and care about its members. On the micro level it is the maternal effect and sentimental approach male managers hold toward their employees.
Animus	Is the Masculine unconscious side in every woman. Once connected to her animus a woman can develop her ambition, career, intellectuality, and physical strength.	Is the Masculine psychic energy and potential activated by a woman manager/employee in order to promote her career, develop innovations, and manage people. In organizations it is the essence of a "Masculine" psychic attitudes.
Conjunction	The unity of opposites (poles like Ying and Yang) refers to sexual intercourse in its spiritual sense.	Any coalition between parties in the organization who come together, join venture, and create new collaborative initiatives.

(Continued)

Table 14.1 (Continued)

Archetype	Individual	Organization
Creation	Human beings' innate creativity that strives to be actualized through arts, science, and wisdom.	The valuable asset of human resources in the research and product developmental sections which concentrates on inventions and innovations. The nuclear of startups.
Destruction	The innate human need to destroy. Freud's Id. Inevitable yet vital asset to achieve change or transformation.	The inevitable unconscious drive in the organization to destruct patterns, initiatives, and sometimes careers.
Ego /Consciousness	Is all what human beings know, aware of, sense, realize, perceive, attribute, and all their deeds.	Is the organizational actual capacity and activities. Is the ability of the organization to acknowledge drawbacks, faults, weaknesses; to hold transparent systems and relationships; and to negotiate freely between teams and managers.
Ego inflation	Is a psychological state where the Ego functioning, behavior and ideas are noticeably increased (like in a state of workaholism), the person is not aware of enlarged self-esteem not fitting reality	Is a malignant situation where the organization's targets, projects, and managerial approaches are far above actual potential to fulfill expectations.
Equilibrium	Human need to balance polarities. The compensatory function that enables human beings stabilize themselves.	Phenomenon aimed to achieve balance and equality between extreme antagonistic powers in the organization.
Heritage	The known history of humankind that inspires innovations, revolutions, and discoveries.	All accumulated knowledge, tradition, and regulations passed in company from generation to generation
Hero	Archetype symbolizes any human quest leaving the security zone and overcoming obstacles that finally entitle him/her not only to proven achievements but spiritual understanding of life as well. Heroism, in Jungian terms, is the psychic work done to transcend the unconscious to consciousness.	Is any employee/manager/ company who dares shift away from the secured position toward a start of a quest in order to upgrade themselves. This quest has steps to go through, although not all are necessarily fulfilled.

(Continued)

Table 14.1 (Continued)

Archetype	Individual	Organization
Individuation	A psychological process human being goes through in the course of becoming who he/she needs to be and become. Is the outcome of the dialogue between the conscious Ego and the unconscious Self.	On the macro level, it is the ability of an organization to actualize its goals, identify its needs and targets, and proceed towards achieving them. On the micro level it is the organization's positive predisposition and policy to enable managers and employees advance, develop, and promote themselves within the organization's boundaries.
Libido	Human beings' sexual drives and energy invested in growth, love, harmony, and integration.	Energy in an organization that enables creativity, affect, communication, and collaboration.
Mythology	The overall legacy of legends, fairytales, and mythologies that convey human traits and needs.	The accumulated organization's memories from its very beginning holding the company's values, history and pride.
Persona	The social mask every human being needs in order to function, includes status, professional markers, garments, skills, and ego maneuvers.	Persona has to do with all external interfaces the organization holds with customers and colleagues: advertisements, logos, icons, organizational uniform, and symbol.
Self	The internal source of inspiration, balancing, and spirituality. The deepest Archetype, "father" of all archetypes, denotes human potential to fulfill and actualize.	The core of the potential growth in organizations, the vision, the company's integrity, the company's future point of view.
Shadow	The inferior side in our personality projected on others. The evil, dark, materialistic, aggressive, jealous, and ugly part in every human being.	Are inferior or evil energies, powers, tendencies, and approaches that dictate the organization's attitude usually on the unconscious level.
Tradition	The culture impact passed on through generations in people and families influencing individual decisions.	The accumulated organizational rituals, habits, and history that dictate the organizational policy.

(Continued)

Table 14.1 (Continued)

Archetype	Individual	Organization
Trickster	Archetype symbolizes the instinctual, manipulative, artistic, clever, political side in human beings.	Is a corporate, manager or employee's talent to manipulate, benefit from weak situations, promote interests, create coalitions and ventures as well as use political acts to benefit chances.
Wounded Healer	An unconscious archetype of healing qualities that all humans possess and is helpful in times of trauma or stress.	Is an experienced wise and creative employee, or consultant who takes over the healing role in the organization. May also be a company's policy or approach.

What is the practical contribution of the archetypal reservoir to a coach who wishes to empower and help to create change in his coachee's performance? The archetype, defined by Samuels (1991), is "evident only through its manifestation". He adds: "they influence a person's functioning ... and are recognizable in outer behaviors ... revealing themselves by way of such inner figures as Anima, Shadow, Persona and so forth" (p. 26). Archetypal patterns, says Samuels, "wait to be realized in the personality". Thus, we are dealing here with *the coachee's unconscious inner psychic image database that presents traits, tales, specific dynamics, and potential.* Once brought into the awareness on the conscious level, an archetype may become a *leading inner coach,* a model for identification, an inner intrinsic active modifying agent for change that transforms and shapes the personality. Stein (1998) backs this by arguing that "to the extent that the archetypes intervene in the shaping of conscious contents by regulating, modifying and motivating them, they act like instincts" (81). This means that if the Jungian coach succeeds to introduce the coachee with a relevant archetype and enables the coachee to identify with it, the archetype will operate on the coachee as an instinct; natural, spontaneous, and real. The archetype is a fantastic role-model engine of traits that the coachee may choose to develop for better professional management or personal behavior. *We may ask, for example, how to encounter a coachee with his or her hidden "trickster" archetype in his or her coachee's managerial proceedings? Why being a trickster is of interest to the coachee at that stage he or she is in the firm? Why is being a trickster paradoxically the very ethical and appropriate response to a certain situation a coachee is challenged with? How will we develop trickster behavior in a coachee's maneuvers? How shall we turn a naïve "by the book" employee who was nominated to a managerial position into someone able to handle the company's strategy as expected when there is much opposition to his nomination?*

The archetypal uniqueness lies in its dual structure, containing opposite values, both negative and positive. Samuels (1985) defines it as: "Archetypal Bipolarity", claiming that "archetypes express a built-in polarity between positive and negative aspects of experience and emotions" (p. 30). With this dual structure, the archetype or image offers our coachees the optimal potential range of behavior choices to choose from, in order to expand toward a desired functioning skill.

Example: The archetype of the Great Mother, which can be referred to as the archetype of the Feminine principle, has two sides. The positive side has to do with nurturing, containing, processing, and repetition. The negative side has to do with instinctual acts, including cruelty, impersonation, and impulse (further explanation in chapter 18). Now an executive senior lady who inherited her fortune and company from her late father walks in his footsteps. At work she can perform from the negative aspect of the Great Mother archetype; she might appear impulsive, instinctual, and react out of a surviving attitude. The Jungian coach, due to her problems in human relationships, may need to help her approximate to the positive side of the Great Mother archetype and get in touch with nurturing, containing, and processing decisions with her subordinates.

Leaning on the "compensatory function" principle, the coachee may choose to adopt an archetypal quality required for better performance. He or she may search for this vital archetypal quality in order to shape it gradually with the support of his or her coach or supportive team. It is about owning a new repertoire of management or performance. At other times, we deal with a potential that needs to be reduced and controlled. This is the case when the client is "possessed" by the archetype (a business woman who is ruled by an evil animus, a housewife mother possessed by maternal rigid guilt feelings, a young businessman possessed by narcissistic ego-me-me archetype, and so on). However, most often the challenge is about what needs to be adapted, nurtured, and increased. Jungian Coaching will become an operative field for practicing and cultivating leaders, managers and employees, as well as companies, to identify the missing archetypal assets they need, connect to them, understand their potential, translate them by actually practicing proven behavior or actions and eventually improving their accomplishments. This process is like the muscles' capacity a coachee is not aware of when first stepping into the Jungian Coaching gym. As he or she persists in practicing on different "machines", he or she will soon develop new "behavioral or managerial muscle tissues" that will shape his or her appearance and performance.

Example: A rumor runs in a company saying that a senior manager harasses his female employees. The company coach is asked to intervene. What preventive intervention must be taken with the manager? Should the manager's undeveloped "Anima" be exposed in order to save both his position and his employees' healthy working environment a moment before catastrophe strikes? This is a most crucial intervention that would bring the manager in contact with his feelings, consider affectionate factors in his response repertoire, and get in touch with his Anima (Feminine side). Let's assume this manager was found as ETSJ on the Mayer-Briggs Preference Test (MBTI) (chapter 29), meaning his personality profile was found as: Extrovert, Thinker, Sensational, and Judgmental. In bringing his inferior functioning to his awareness and using his auxiliary/tertiary capacities (Feeling – Intuitive sides) to prevent him from abusive behavior, we grant him a chance for an eloquent change. This is where the scholar, authoritarian highly qualified manager will have to befriend with his inferiority; "Anima" archetype (emotional database), discover and explore it, dialogue with it, and take it under consideration in his daily strategies and behavior at the office.

Bolen (1989) compares the archetypes to a "DNA program" of seeds. "The sprouts depend upon the soil and climate, the presence or lack of certain nurturing ingredients loving or negligent gardeners, the size and depth of the container and the courage of the species themselves are preliminary conditions to connect to an archetype. Archetypes are basic human structures. Some are manifested already from early childhood's tendency, for example musical talents, psychic maturity, motor coordination or intellect. Same with archetypal structures; some people minister their archetypal structure from early childhood and some may discover their archetypal traits in the middle of life, if they fall in love, for example, they very likely will discover Dionysus" (26) the lover archetype.

In Jungian Coaching we work with the whole spectrum of the bipolar archetypal repertoire; therefore, it is crucial to understand the theoretical psychic dual polar structure of the archetypes. Every archetype has its "positive" and "negative" traits, yet each duality contains multiple ranges of archetypes, which look to me like a Japanese fan. "Mother Archetype" (Jung 1969, p. 21), for instance, bears the birth-giving and nurturing element of life's existence on the one pole. At the same time, the "Mother Archetype" may present a captive, cannibal, or destructive experience (symbolized in mythologies as Kali the goddess of death or a suffocating cave) at the opposing pole. In between we may find all the varieties of maternal symbolic presentations: arrogancy, intervening, manipulative, and sexually seductive, which eventually reaches to positive aspects of educating, comforting, role gender positive leader, etc.

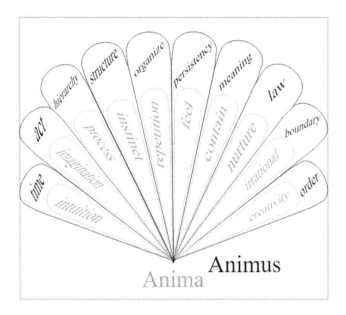

Figure 14.1 Japanese Fans of Anima and Animus.

This is an example illustrating the various aspects of the Feminine (Anima) and Masculine (Animus) archetypal principles that will be explained in chapters 18–19.

Jung's collaboration and friendship with the theoretical physicist and Nobel Prize winner Wolfgang Pauli deepened and validated Jung's understanding of the Archetypes and their bipolar characteristics in the human psyche. They found out an analogy between Planck's Quantum Mechanism (1858–1947) and the opposing duality not only of the archetypes but also of consciousness versus unconsciousness, the Ego in relations to the Self, the Ego versus the Shadow and the complementary aspects of the Anima/Animus in relations to the Ego's genders. Jung and Pauli validated those psychic mechanisms relying on the physics statement about the duality of the particle spin in quantum physics. Accordingly, the two particle's spin are always correlated (opposite), *meaning the electron can have an upward and downward spin simultaneously* existing in both states in parallel, until measured, and causing the "Uncertainty Principle". The Uncertainty Principle, also called the "Heisenberg uncertainty principle" (1927) is further elaborated on by the German physicist Werner Heisenberg, who proved that the position and the velocity of an object cannot both be measured exactly, at the same time. Their findings created the theoretical rationale for the four Jungian principles described previously (chapter 6 & 7: *the flipping principle*).

Every dilemma is "sited" in hidden archetypes. The beginning of a coaching process starts by using the "transcendent function technique". This technique clarifies which archetype is connected, associates, or involved with the topic we focus on. Or, alternately, which archetype the coachee should connect to in order to discover the powers required for gaining his or her targets. Sometimes it will be the client who will produce a symbol or image to work with, and other times it might be the coach who will offer a technique, coaching game, or card to empower the coachee.

The transcendent function is that mental process that occurs while dreaming, creating art, or free associating. Unconscious material finds its way out to the conscious level. According to Jung it "transcends" the Ego as the archetypal content both enriches and challenges the Ego and by this empowers the Ego consciousness. In order to connect with a relevant archetype, we need to encourage the coachee to associate with an image that relates to or expresses the dilemma he or she wishes to focus on (chapter 8). This paradoxical distancing from the "issue at coaching" toward an artistic or creative association, image, or symbol will eventually bring up an unconscious clue that will approximate an archetype (chapter 4). As shown previously in Table 14.1 we may use the basic archetypes upon which we can establish effective Jungian Coaching on both the individual and company levels. Once the relevant archetype has been sorted out, it is applied, and experientially practiced, for the sake of the coachee's needs. In the Jungian Coaching method, we developed a kit of games and cards that helps the client connect to targeted archetypes according to various life and business challenges. *Example: Edna, age 47, a successful CEO in a very large production company, is referred to coaching for severe outbursts of temper resulting in attacks on her subordinates, behavior that could well damage her career. She is a pretty and energetic woman who creates an immediate and good rapport with the coach. A 20-minute intake interview exposes the following data: she is the second child after a mentally challenged brother, her mother was neglected by her father while pregnant with her, her father left for good to another country, her mother returned to the village and back to the big city with her grandmother (mom's mother) and an alcoholic uncle (no positive male figures to identify with). Life in the big city offers her two options during her childhood and youth: grow up as a juvenile delinquent or connect to her Animus and make a brilliant career – which she did, getting a PhD and relocating to faraway countries. She marries a businessman and brings up two children. She works from 7:00 to 20:00 assisted by helpers at home, while her husband is away at work. She was nominated general manager; however, the firm accountant, long before her in the company, ran his financial activities arrogantly ignoring her and retaining direct contact with the owners; as a result, she is outraged. The coach's impression was that the coachee is "Animus possessed". She is not using her Feminine assets (patience, nurturing, mediating, affectionate, processing) and her righteousness drives her crazy. The coach suggests that she work with clay (transcendent function). Using her hands, Edna first squeezes the clay with her fists toward the hard table (as she does to the accountant). After feedback, she changes the clay position upward and, while caressing it, she shapes it tenderly into a huge arc. Now Edna is relaxed. She is asked to hold a dialogue between herself and the sculpture. She praises the sculpture-mountain and wishes to rest in its curves; the mountain invites her in. She carves holes (columbarium) inside, practicing Feminine nesting (for retreating). She discusses with the coach the essential need to regain Feminine qualities in her managerial interactions; she looks for ideas. The coach brings two miniatures: a goddess connected to mother-earth and a hero/knight. She locates them in relationship with the holy mountain, and there is a discussion between the knight and the goddess; two qualities essential for her best management skills. They agree to meet in a few weeks for a follow-up.*

Figure 14.2 Goddess and Knight.

The difference between common coaching and Jungian Coaching is in its archetypal use. The Jungian coach learns to identify the psychodynamic archetypal contents of the archetypes involved in the coachee's dilemma. He or she practices with the coachee now to achieve the expected skills or changes targeted by the coachee.

In shifting from intellectual analysis into practical coaching experiential training, I find that D. E. Kalsched's (2019) innovative lecture inspires the Jungian Coaching. This Jungian contemporary analyst recently shared a personal "wishing memory" from his own analysis in the Vienna Congress of Jungian Psychology: "Look" (*he imagines his analyst would have told him*) "let's just slow down for a moment – close your eyes, and let yourself sink into your body – just relax, follow your breath and pay attention to any sensations, images or feelings that come up. Just notice the felt sense of what you're experiencing. Had something painful emerged, he *(his idealized analyst,)* might have asked me where I felt it in my body, and he would have asked me to stay with it – not move back into my head, as I so want to do. He might have handed me paper and crayons and had me draw my feelings. He might have helped me with a guided imagination instead of sending me home to do active imagination by myself with an imagination that had already dried up" (p. 5). We can conclude that in coaching any archetypal training requires experiential practice.

This is how the "Complex" concept synergies here. Complex is a "mixture" of several archetypes that connect unconsciously and create strong emotional reactions. Stein (1998) explains that:

> There are indeed psychic entities outside of consciousness, which exist as satellite-like objects in relations to the ego-conscious but are able to cause ego disturbances in a surprising and sometimes overwhelming way. They are the gremlins and inner demons that may catch a person by surprise. (34)

If we analyzed Edna's (the businesswoman from the recent example) irrational complex behavior for which she referred herself to coaching, we may discover that her misconduct as a CEO derived from what we term in Jungian Psychology as a "Complex". The finance manager "constellated" her. "The term 'constellation'", claims Stein (1998), "refers to the creation of a psychologically charged moment, a moment when consciousness either already is, or is about to become, disturbed by a complex" (36). Complexes are a cluster-blended unconscious contents, expressed as archetypes at its core, to which humans react with strong emotions. They belong to the autonomous unconscious; although constant, they are universal and display themselves on the "personal level" in thinking, feeling, and kinesthetic forms.

The psychic mechanism of "Complex" is relevant to coaching because it helps assess our clients' manifested problem, their hidden motivations, and the patterns of their complicated relationships. Edna had an "Animus Complex", which is a mixture of her personal story with men *(mentally challenged brother, mother is neglected by father while pregnant, father leaves for good, and an alcoholic uncle enters her life instead)* blended with "undeveloped Femininity" *(lack of patience, nurturing, mediating, affectionate, processing)*. When those two energies fused with the archetype of "Destruction" *(the innate human need to destroy. Freud's Id. Inevitable yet vital asset to achieve change or transformation)* she could have either jeopardized her career or alternatively arrived at coaching. Stein (1998) validates this observation by adding that "Jung describes 'complex' as being made up of associated images and frozen memories of traumatic moments that are buried in the unconscious and not readily available for retrieval by the ego" (44).

While working with archetypes we need to keep in mind Stein's (1998) comments that "archetypes have, when they appear, a distinctly numinous character which can only be described as 'spiritual', if 'magical' is too strong a word". He adds: "it can be healing or destructive, but never indifferent, provided of course that it has a certain degree of clarity" (82). In coaching, while activating the archetypes chosen or picked up by the client, we should be cautious because "when the ego comes upon an archetypal image, it may become possessed by it, overwhelmed, and give up even wanting to resist, for the experience feels so rich and meaningful" (82). This is my experience as a Jungian coach, often the client reports about revelation, innovation, and curiosity. My clients and students keep saying:"it is so deep and so fast!"

Chapter 15

Holistic approach: Ego (conscious), Self (unconscious) and the Ego–Self Axis

"That 'other spirit' forces me nevertheless to speak, beyond justification, use and meaning".

Red Book, Liber Primus (pg. 229)

The Ego (which corresponds to the coachee's acts), the conscious level (meaning, what the coachee knows and aware of), the Self (which is the coachee's internal knowledge, spirituality and hidden assets as well as his or her whole total being), and his or her unconscious (the parts in the coachee's psyche which are hidden) are conceived in Jungian Coaching as the whole coachee's personality.

The Jungian coaching approach offers an ongoing intellectual and emotional effort in assimilating unconscious materials of the coachee to his or her conscious awareness and acts. Therefore, in Jungian Coaching we should always bear in mind the fraction: *conscious/unconscious.* Stein (1998) argues that "consciousness is what we know, the unconsciousness is all that we do not know" (13). The Collective Unconscious, as definded by C.G Jung, claims Stein (1998) is "the deepest layer of the human psyche... which is conceived of its contents as a combination of universally prevalent patterns and forces called 'archetypes' and 'instincts'" (72). Practically, this calls for listening to the coachee's argument, story, or dilemma and at the same time reflect on the unconscious and collective unconscious layers that accompany the coachee's text. When people face a dilemma, they search automatically for practical solutions and comforting advice from previous experiences, sticking to what they were accustomed to, holding onto familiar capacities or assets that had been available in their nearby environment. The coachee's available knowledge, skills, experiences, logical mind, and common sense, as well as physical sensations and emotions, all those are considered in Jungian Coaching as the coachee's *Conscious Mind.* The Ego is the "hero" of consciousness. Consciousness includes the potential of a person to analyze, differentiate, and integrate data and feelings and relate to all cognitive and affective functions. The client's *Ego* (which corresponds to the conscious mind) is considered the overt daily functioning activities with which the coachee

DOI: 10.4324/9780429351518-15

operates in the world (personal and professional). Stein (1998) claims that "the ego is a focal point within consciousness, its most central and perhaps most permanent feature" (15). Kast (1992) adds that "some of the primary autonomous ego functions are: sensation, thought, attention, the ability to perceive, the capacity to remember, the formation of concepts, orientation in time and space, motor functions, and also defense mechanism" (p. 67). In an *"Ego inflated"* state, the Ego functions are noticeably and exaggeratedly increased (as in the state of workaholics), and the person is not aware of this enlarged self-esteem or swollen expectations that do not match reality.

We could use Stein's (1998) metaphor for the Ego as "a mirror or magnet that holds contents in a focal point of awareness" (15) and argue that the "Corporate's Ego" has to do with its actual productivity, revenue, and loss; the ability of the company to acknowledge drawbacks, faults, weaknesses, to hold transparent systems and relationships; and to negotiate freely between teams and directors. We shall consider a "corporate Ego Inflated state" as any malignant situation where a company's targets, projects, and managerial approaches are far above actual potential to fulfill expectations. In Jungian Coaching we assess first, the "Ego functioning potential" of our client/corporation and then we plan the coaching assignments according to the coachee or client's *Ego Forces*. The aim of Jungian Coaching is to stimulate the coachee's unconscious in order to expand and strengthen the boundaries of his or her consciousness, and this is ministered by assimilating the unconscious content's reservoir into consciousness. Yet, "the Ego's freedom is limited", says Stein (1998), "it is easily influenced by both internal psychic and external environmental stimuli" (17).

The *Unconscious* is considered in Jungian Coaching as a huge reservoir of psychic potential that lies hidden within the coachee's or corporate's psyche.

Jung (1983), in his famous book *Memories, Dreams & Reflections*, presents his dream that validated his innovative concept of the Unconscious. The dream unfolds as follows:

> I was in a house I did not know, which had two storeys. It was "my house." I found myself in the upper storey, where there was a kind of salon furnished with fine old pieces in rococo style. On the walls hung a number of precious old paintings. I wondered if this should be my house, and thought, "Not bad." But then it occurred to me that I did not know what the lower floor looked like. Descending the stairs, I reached the ground floor. There everything was much older, and I realised that this part of the house must date from about the fifteenth or sixteenth century. The furnishings were medieval; the floors were of red brick. Everywhere it was rather dark. I went from one room to another, thinking, "Now I really must explore the whole house." I came upon a heavy door, and opened it. Beyond it, I discovered a stone stairway that led down into the cellar. Descending again, I found myself in a beautifully vaulted room which looked exceedingly ancient. Examining the walls, I discovered

layers of brick among the ordinary stone blocks, and chips of brick in the mortar. As soon as I saw this I knew that the walls dated from Roman times. My interest by now was intense. I looked more closely at the floor. It was on stone slabs, and in one of these I discovered a ring. When I pulled it, the stone slab lifted, and again I saw a stairway of narrow stone steps leading down into the depths. These, too, I descended, and entered a low cave cut into the rock. Thick dust lay on the floor, and in the dust were scattered bones and broken pottery, like remains of a primitive culture. I discovered two human skulls, obviously very old and half disintegrated. Then I awoke. (p. 182)

This dream teaches us about the Conscious–Unconscious topographic location in our client's psyche. "The unconscious includes all the psychic contents that lie outside of consciousness, for whatever reason and whatever duration" (Stein, 1998, 13). The unconscious conceives archetypal images and symbols and the deepest and most prominent archetype in the unconscious is the 'Self'. Kast (1992) describes the Self archetype as "the creative principle that guides the structuring of the Ego complex. It is the psyche's self-regulation" (p. 5). She mentions that "the symbols of the Self, as Jung said, arise in the depths of the body; they express both our materiality and the structure of the perceiving consciousness" (p. 5). Kast specifies that "the Self can be represented by abstract symbols, such as the circle, sphere, triangle or cross, they symbolize wholeness and characteristically contain many opposites as they are not necessarily merged" (p. 5). There are several "Self" symbols; the light, because it brings knowledge and clarity to the Ego. The light illuminates the "ignorant darkness". Accompanying the light is the Sun. Beside illuminating and adding transparency, the sun nurtures life through photosynthesis, and because the sun rays are fast, the sun is attributed to the Masculine principle: rapid, linear, and dwells in the "spiritual sky" (chapter 19). The "Self" is also a symbol for development, because the more we grow and advance, the bigger our "Self" becomes. In "Self" symbolism, we shall find the egg, the baby, the baby Buddha sitting on lotus leaves, the Christ child or Moses in a cradle, and the innocent. They all symbolize potential, which, in future, creates heroes, geniuses, leaders and prophets, and so on. Another symbol of the "Self", which correlates with potential, is Gold, which is considered, in alchemical texts, as the utmost metal among all the metals, and the treasure which is a condensed potential. In addition, every vehicle of transportation, which promotes the hero on its quest, such as a boat, wings, fire (Jupiter), horse, engine, or airplane, are all symbols of "Self" transformation. Of high importance for "Self" symbolism stands the Mandala, which Jung found to be a deep "Self" meditative spiritual balancing artistic activity. He displays and writes of its importance in his *Red Book* (2009). The Mandala organizes the Ego around a balanced structure. Anatomically, we are built as a unit with a symmetrical body structure. Our head begins a vertical sequence that terminates with our soles. We are also balanced through twin symmetrical organs. Every artistic organized expression hints toward a balanced experience. Obviously, the deliberate breakdown of the balance may be an artistic statement. Apparently, one of the characteristics of the "Self" is an absolute symmetry, balance, and centering locus. It denotes perfection. When the opposites in our personality are integrated into one unity, we arrive at a balanced tranquil life experience. Samuels (1985) contributes further to our understanding of the Jungian "Self". He explains that for Jung the "'Self' helps discover the meaning and purpose in life" (p. 89), "it's special function is *to balance* and pattern not only the other archetypes, *but all of a person's life in terms of purpose as yet unconsidered and unlived"* (p. 92). Practically, the concept of the Jungian "Self" is the Jungian coach's and coachee's conductor and compass. When a coachee refers to coaching, from a Jungian coaching point of view, he or she actually searches to connect to his or her internal leader, to listen to a deep intuitive wisdom, which has the cognitive, emotional, and sensational know-how. Further Samuels (1985) adds: "the Self is synthesizer and mediator of opposites within the psyche … self-regulatory and healing nature" (p. 92). According to Samuels (1985), other symbols of the Self include "any feeling of integration, coupled with a sense of place in the scheme of things; the personality is enriched".

The coach, as well as the coachee, highly likely will find it very challenging to trust the Self missives brought through the archetypal symbols that arise during the Jungian coaching session. Stein (1998) claims that "the unconscious is at least potentially available to the Ego, even if the Ego does not ever actually experience much of it" (21). In Jungian Coaching, in the presence of a dilemma the coachee brought up, we can advise the coachee to draw one *concrete drawing* that represents a dilemma the coachee is intrigued with. According to Goren-Bar (2019, pp. 86–103) Concrete drawing would derive from the conscious-mind (the Ego domain). Then, ask the client to draw an *abstract* drawing (which derives from the depth of the unconscious), and finally ask the client to hold a *dialogue* between the Ego and the Self as they are presented in the drawings. We must heed carefully to the Ego–Self dialogue in the context of the choachee's dilemma. Art that is inspired by the "Ego level" is concrete and conscious: it is comprehensible, obvious, and anybody can figure out what the client meant to express. Usually the contents of concrete arts are overt experiences that the client observed in real life, and the rules of physics and common sense are dominant. Unlike Ego art, the arts that derive from the "Self" level are abstract. They are open to interpretation or require explanation. Surrealism is one example of this style. They are ruled by imagination and transmit a metaphor very likely not realistic. Such arts cause us to associate, project, and merge into the artistic production, bringing our own subjective comprehension to them. A theoretical rationale for the coaching practice of *Ego-Self artistic dialogue* can be found in Stein's (1998) comment claiming that: "although 'wholeness' seems at first sight to be nothing but an abstract idea, it is nevertheless empirical in so far as it is anticipated by the psyche in the form of spontaneous or autonomous symbols" (129). The coach should ask the coachee to choose in the Self abstract artifact a part that possibly can contribute to the Ego-dilemma's drawing. Ask what that part in the Self drawing symbolizes, and how it can possibly contribute to further comprehending the dilemma. There will always be a valuable insight on the client's awareness of that dilemma (Figure 15.1).

Figure 15.1 Ego-Self Dialogue – Dilemma.

Example: She is an architect and hates her job (Ego drawing). In the Ego drawing she drew an urban view which is associated with her architectural sketchings done daily at her work. Her "Self's" abstract drawing displays a spontaneous impulsive blue gouache blot. In the dialogue between the Ego and the Self drawings the Ego drawing says: "I am too structured, too rigid, cold, detached, not human although people live inside me". The Self says: "I am blue, I can become a beautiful lake flowing in your main street". Coach: "What does blue symbolize for you?" Coachee: "Spirituality, definitely spirituality, like heaven". Coach: "How can you incorporate spirituality into your architectural job?" Coachee says:"I have been thinking of going to study art therapy". She cuts out a piece of the blue blot and integrates it in the Ego drawing (Figure 15.2).

Figure 15.2 Ego-Self Dialogue – Solution.

Jungian Coaching offers tools and techniques to connect conscious dilemmas to unconscious potential solutions and then practice their actualization. The *Self* in Jungian Coaching is considered an inner inspiration and internal wisdom to which the coachee is expected to connect and listen. Jung said that the Ego to the Self is analogous to Men and God. Unlike the Ego, the Self is taken in Jungian Coaching as the power of imagination, the source for innovative ideas, and the endless intrinsic support one can obtain from within. Unlike the Ego, the Self might be irrational, terribly powerful, and usually challenging. Through Jungian Coaching, the coachee learns to heed to the Self and obtain (through the principle of the *Transcendent*

Function) ideas and directions for innovative problem solving. Jungian Coaching functions as a practical consulting approach by establishing an effective Ego-Self working axis. Kast (1992) says that "The relationship between the Self and the Ego is based on reciprocation" (p. 6) (Figure 15.3).

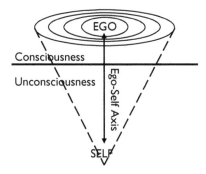

Figure 15.3 Ego-Self Axis.

Jungian coaching dwells in the dreaming and creating psychic zone. As seen in Figure 15.4, the stimulus of the Jungian coaching techniques will invite the coachee into nonrational symbolic experiences. The dilemma that the client brings up in the coaching session eventually takes the client to the domain of imagination and creativity where the Self overlaps part of the Ego (in Figure 15.4 it is the third option from the left). This psychic position may cause anxiety, resistance, or curiosity and enthusiasm, depending on the client's mechanism of defense, motivation for change, and Ego strength.

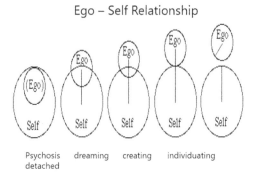

Figure 15. 4 Ego in Relations to Self, "The Cycle of Growth" by Brian T. Baulsom M.N.I.S.H.

In the threshold between consciousness and unconsciousness rests the person's or the organization's subjective truth. *Part of every manifested life or organizational story will always derive from two sources: the "personal" that represents the conscious known and well aware background of the client, and the compensating, diminishing, or overwhelming irrational archetypal addition, which is presented in the story without necessarily a direct connection to the event.* Samuels (1985) reflects on the origin of the Ego-Self Axis: "The ego-self axis (which is a term coined by Neumann, but used with greater precision by Edinger) functions as a gateway between the conscious parts of the personality *(the coachee's issues, questions, problems)* and the unconscious *(the coachee's internal wisdom)*" (p. 116) (Figure 15.5).

PERSONAL

ARCHETYPAL

Figure 15.5 Personal in Relation to Archetypal.

This turns Jungian Coaching into a very exciting and intriguing experience, as the Jungian coach will not just take the reported story of the coachee for granted, will never remain on the reported testimonial text, but rather will seek out the complex unique blend of the archetypal level of the story and how it possibly contributes to the conscious mind of the client's (individual or organization) argument. Kast (1992) reinforces this approach by claiming that:

> In order to come into contact with the complexes, or with the disturbances (and I should add with the coachee's expectation to cope with a dilemma he or she actually goes with blindly) we must consider the fantasy, dreams, patterns of relationships, and symbols as relevant factors as well. Since complexes can be worked out in fantasy, we have an opportunity to transform them from inhibiting forces to encouraging forces. This is what happens in symbolization. (p. 40)

Jungian Coaching therefore establishes a "practical Ego-Self Axis" where the client, with the help of the coach, pulls out unconscious material and assimilates it on the conscious overt behavior level.

Chapter 16

Alchemy – create change

"On your journey be sure to take golden cups full of the sweet drink of life, red wine, and give it to dead matter, so that it can win life back".

Red Book, Liber Primus (pg. 244)

In this chapter we present how the esoteric ideas that Jung found in Alchemy can serve as different coaching attitudes toward change. Coaching deals finally with a wish for change. In Alchemical Studies, Jung (1967) writes: "This was in 1928. I had been investigating the processes of the collective unconscious since 1913 and had obtained results that seemed to me questionable in more than one respect" (3). This was a lifetime investigation into what seemed like irrational pseudo sciences that intrigued Jung and gave us eventually the well-known *Red Book* (Published in 2009) with deep and widespread knowledge about symbolism and the collective unconscious. Samuels (1985) writes about Alchemy that "the alchemists described many of the problems of modern psychology in their own language and Jung felt that they had intuitively anticipated and imaginatively projected what has been verified in modern times" (p. 179). Netzer (2004), a prominent Israeli Jungian analyst and my mentor, dedicates a book to the Alchemy of the Soul and the Alchemy Process. When she specifies the stages of the alchemy process, she demonstrates the amazing parallel between metal versus mental processes (p. 173). Those descriptions of change processors are relevant to Jungian Coaching, which is change-oriented. Often the coach and coachee avoid direct change approach because those do not come without suffering (Goren-Bar, 2018, pp. 16–22). Netzer (2004) counts seven alchemical processes to obtain substantial change:

The first technique for changing a substance is *"Kalkinatio"* meaning in Latin, burning, melting, drying, changing into dust and warming by fire. If translated into a coaching approach (think of the original coaching athletes) this means to encourage the coachee to accelerate, work harder, add more hours of investment and effort and do more in order to increase

DOI: 10.4324/9780429351518-16

outcomes. When the "Pizza", Ego forces, is weak or narrow we should consider the option of the Kalkinatio approach with the client. We must encourage the coachee to invest more effort, more trials, more attempts in order to achieve the desired goal. *Example: A young talented man graduated from the Body-Psyche Medical school and wishes to start private practice. He is shy and insecure and arrives at coaching with the wish to find advice on how to recruit clients. According to the Kalkinatio approach he is required to make a long list of friends and contacts and call them to bring to their awareness the fact that he has opened a clinic, prepare personal card and handle it to as many people as possible, show attempts to be invited to t.v and radio programs to expose his talents and added value.* (Using the Masculine Principle cards, chapter 19 would be very helpful.)

The second is *Solutio,* which refers to melting the solid with water. In Jungians terms this means melting the conscious mechanisms into unconsciousness and emotions. When the coachee is too cognitive, thinks, estimates, and calculates too much while the change requires reconsiderations that include emotions and sentimental and irrational data to be included in the equation, we need to consider involving the Solutio principle. In the Hero Quest (chapter 25) we may find the stage of "Crossing the Threshold" as an efficient experience for reconsidering emotions in a cognitive decision making. In addition, connecting to the Feminine Principle (chapter 18) is also advisable in the Solutio approach to change. *Example: After thirty years of marriage a man comes to coaching with a decision he cannot commit: he is in parallel relationships with a woman who demands (as much as he wants to) that he divorce his wife and move to live with her. In coaching the guy is drawn into calculations and rationalizations (consciousness) avoiding himself totally from emotions (Unconsciousness, Anima). In Solutio, meeting with his emotions (through active imagination in a dialogue with his Anima) will very likely give him insight and energy to move his life forwards.*

The third technique for change is *Kagulatio,* meaning drying. Drying out the material from the emotional water and turning the liquid material into substantial, grounding, practical consideration. This attitude stands in opposition to the previous approach. If the coachee is hysterical, in panic, too emotional, too ambitious, too involved, or too enthusiastic, it is advisable to adopt the Kagulatio approach, meaning learn to set aside the emotional stuff and act rationally. In the Kagulatio approach for change holding on to the Masculine Principle (chapter 19) is advisable. On the Hero Quest this experience will correspond to the stage of "Atonement with the Father".

Example: A woman with very creative and spiritual talents, went on early retirement from a job where she was employed for many years doing clerk work. Now she wishes to start a new business based on a healing approach.

She is brainstormed with ideas, restless and terribly enthusiastic yet can not organize a business plan and prioritize her schedule. Kagulatio approach will lead her to a step by step structured plan which will help this woman transmit ideas into work.

The fourth stage is *Sublimatio,* meaning vaporization, transforming the impulsive concrete behavior into the spiritual and the symbolic. When the client reaches high materialistic achievements and has no spiritual tendency to balance his life experience, he might fall into moods, depression or addictions. Such states are represented on the Hero Quest (chapter 25) at the stages of "The Woman as Temptress" and "Crossing of the Return Threshold". Sublimation connects to the principle of Materialistic vs. Spirituality (chapter 6) and is applied in the business world during negotiations, collaborations, and partnerships. *Example: The Israeli Kibbutz Hatzerim in the Desert of Negev owns the royalty for the world's known irrigation system technique called "Taftafot", first invented in the 1970s. A dripping pipe turns the desert into paradise. This invention turned the socially modest communal settlement into a very rich Kibbutz. Their concern was not to become materialistically inflated, and they found philanthropic projects to invest their money. One of their Sublimation project investments was "Kedma", a village for delinquent youth.*

The fifth is *Mortification*, Death. Every move from one stage into another in life, any transformation or change, inevitably kills its previous existing presence, turning the present into past with possible death experiences (metaphoric or actual). So is the Mortification/Negrado that deals with darkness, rot, decomposition, suffering, and inventible torture. Coachees who are involved with business, relationship, studies, as well as life events, when facing an end, must acquire an ability to let go of the past and enable new changes to take over. This is where Mortification needs to be applied and accepted. *Example: a young enthusiastic and talented man has qualified himself to become a certified tourist guide in Chinese. With the Corona pandemic his career was dead early in February of 2020. He fell deep into Mortification, a process that took five months. After elaborating the trauma, needing to take care of his family (his wife is a chef who lost her job as restaurants were locked down as well), he started to search for an alternative job. This he could not have done before he lamented on his lost desired career as he loved Chinese. He found a job as customer service technician in a startup that works intensively with the Chinese market and eventually started a new career.*

The sixth is *Seperatio*, means to separate, cut, differentiate, distillate, and pull apart the material from all what is irrelevant, sort things out by conscious analytic work. When the client is facing too many ideas, overwhelmed by creative initiatives, in a time of chaos or when business is in real difficulties, the coachee must be helped to put facts and data in priority. This is a Seperatio assignment. Here the Masculine (chapter 19) psychic database in the coachee's toolbox is advisable. The Seperation technique correlates with the Kalkinatio. *Example: a successful executive is offered a relocation; however, too many contradicting factors are involved in his considerations. In addition his wife gets pregnant and his three-year-old son is diagnosed on the spectrum. This person arrives at coaching with despair and desperately needs to put order, priorities, and pros and cons considerations before approaching his wife to decide whether to accept or deny the proposal. Separation is the required approach in such a case.*

The seventh, and the last, technique to acquire change is *Conjunctio.* *Conjunction* refers to the connection between polarities and bringing resources into integration. Change can become fruitful if the coachee can benefit from contradicting elements, contradicting partners, and opposing interests. How to bridge and mediate is at the heart of the Conjunctio principle. *Example: synergy between two competing companies is one of the most challenging merges in the corporate world. After years of tough competition, cynicism, and over patronizing, the human resource managers must display intense and profound work to build up "bridges of collaborations". At the same time the finance managers are expected to set up a suitable budget for the merging process. There must be a period of conjunctio activities in the companies to arrive to a decent merging.*

In the Corona pandemic crisis our clients may need to consider all those alchemical approaches to be helped out. (chapter 32).

Chapter 17

The Persona archetype: About interfaces

"You wear the mask of a devil, a frightful one, the mask of the banal, of eternal mediocrity…is the struggle with this mask worthwhile? Was the mask of God worth worshiping?".

Red Book, Liber Primus (pg. 241)

In the next chapters we shall survey a gallery of practical archetypes to which the individuals or corporation are expected to connect to gain significant changes. "The Persona and Shadow archetypes are complementary structures", claims Stein (1998), "and exist in every developed human psyche" (86).

Persona is named after the Roman term for an actor's mask. This archetype is considered the closest to the conscious level, meaning it is the *social performing mask we "wear" every morning when we get to work or set out to life activities.* Persona includes all the corporation's interfaces with the "outer world"; customers, providers, competitors, collaborators, and associates. Persona has to do with fashion, personal taste, marketing, branding, advertisement, the executive's symbols of status, the design of the office (open space vs. closed secretary battalion indoor office), personal card, proclaimed statement of belief, the corporate uniform, personal items, gadgets, icons, your bag, your car, your travel agent, your personal assistant, your friends, your club, and so many more. Google, Facebook, Instagram, LinkedIn, TikTok, and others are all "agents" functioning in the service of the Persona archetype. In the Corona pandemic Persona issues connect to the Zoom appearance, Zoom communication for better and worse (chapter 32). Obviously, billions are invested on the Persona level. Often, the Jungian coach is expected to intervene on this level "out there" to evoke change as the Persona is indeed the external layer in which significant changes are eventually manifested. Even more so, sometimes mere changes on the Persona level will cause significant changes on much deeper levels. An example for radical change on Persona level (gender) for beneficial outcome is manifested in the film *Yentl*, 1983 (USA), directed by Barbra Streisand,

DOI: 10.4324/9780429351518-17

where a Jewish girl disguises herself as a boy and enters an orthodox school and falls in love with Avigdor, her classmate.

As "the Persona is the person that we become as a result of acculturation, education, and adaptation to our physical and social environments" (Stein, 1998, 89), I would like to discuss here a challenging aspect of the Persona archetype and its relevance to coaching. When Jung (1982) presents his ideas about Femininity and the Anima, he first deliberately presents the Persona and argues its positive and negative aspects: "A compensatory relationship exists between Persona and Anima", he states. How does this relate to coaching? Because the Persona grants us safeties often within fake security zones (habitual arrogance and illusion) and because the Persona is connected to social standards and society's norms, Jung warns the reader from the Persona, "enemy of change", which is awaiting "out there" as an obstacle for change. Here is an existential paradox: the Persona, on the one hand, provides us with social stability and gratifications but at the same time turns out paradoxically to be preventing the client from executing significant change, prohibiting the coachee from not only modifying his life but even thinking about possible modifications. This reciprocity between the Persona archetype and other "Archetypal-Change-Activators" is very crucial in comprehending the intrinsic challenge of the Jungian Coaching processes. To put it simply we may say that although the coachee comes to coaching, expresses motivation, and intention to change and gain significant achievements, when it comes to issues such as prestige, cost, popularity – all which are Persona aspects – he or she shows hesitance, antagonism, concerns, and fears. Apparently Jung himself clarifies this practical dilemma very brightly in his own words:

> The Persona is a complicated system of relationships between the individual consciousness and society, fittingly enough a kind of mask, designed on the one hand to make a definite impression upon others, and on the other hand, to conceal the true nature of the individual. One who is so identified with his personal that he no longer knows himself; and what the former unnecessary can only occur to one who is quite unconscious of the true nature of his fellows. Society expects, and indeed must expect every individual to play the part assigned to him as perfectly as possible, so that a man who is a parson must not only carry out the official functions objectively, but must at all times and in all circumstances play the role of parson in a flawless manner ... each must stand at his post ... otherwise such a man would be "different" from other people, not quite reliable. (p. 82)

Jung goes on:

> Construction of an artificial personality becomes an unavoidable necessity...what goes on behind the masks then called "private life" ... the construction of collectively suitable Persona means a formidable concession

to the external world, a genuine self-sacrifice which drives the ego straight into identification with the Persona. (p. 83)

Here is where Jung approaches coaching and therapy: "These identifications with a social role are a very fruitful source of neuroses. *A man cannot get rid of himself in favor of an artificial personality without punishment"*. Jung quotes Lao-tzu: "High rests on law". Meaning: "An opposite force its way up from inside; it is exactly as though the unconscious suppressed the ego with the very same power which drew the Ego into the Persona."

In the Jungian Coaching practice with Persona (on executive and individual life coaching) one should start first with the Pizza analysis, meaning the clients' activities and interface with society. If the client's self-esteem is law, if the activities are impressive but the profit or outcome is poor, if the marketing and public relations are insufficient, if the client's appearance or his body language does not fit, then soft skills techniques are required to strengthen the Persona.

On the corporate level, one possible example for "Persona wrong decision-making process" is Janis's (1982) phenomenon of "GroupThink", a misperception of the competitors deriving from self-righteousness. Wrong branding, recurring productions with poor creative or non-innovative products, "old fashion" styles, and traditional rigid standards or strict regulations are sorts of Persona failures. *The Founder*, a 2016 American biographical comedy-drama film about McDonald's directed by John Lee Hancock, makes a good example for Persona considerations as well as Trickster archetypal maneuvers. In chapter 32 we shall analyze in detail the effect of the Corona pandemic on the Persona, Shadow, and Anima archetypes.

Chapter 18

The Anima/Feminine archetype: Deepening inwards

"If you are boys, your God is a woman. If you are woman, your God is a boy. If you are men, your God is a maiden. The God is where you are not."

Red Book, Liber Primus (pg. 234)

According to Denise (1997) in The Feminine in the Foundations of Organizational Psychology, modern Western society with its high-tech and industrialized mass productions, accompanied by computing IT (Information Technology), is characterized, from a Jungian Coaching point of view, as dominated by the Masculine Principle. In presenting the complementary Feminine Principle, and by applying it to coaching skills, we acquire a balancing approach that can contribute to better management among both men and women.

As we saw in the previous chapter, the archetypes can interweave: Persona connected to the Anima, which here connects to the Shadow. Recall the Moses sculpture by Michelangelo, San Pietro in Rome, you would remember he holds two tablets. In Jungian Coaching both *Anima (Animus)* and the *Shadow* archetypes hold together the ten commandments of the Jungian Coaching method.

As a psychiatrist, son to a family with six priests, Jung was a "Western" and was raised up by the western idea that the world had been created by God, the divine creator, the initiator, planner, organizer, all powerful and knowledgeable. In the Western approach the world is metaphorically a clock, God is clock-watcher, the architect. Human role is to analyze the clock. Psychoanalysis is a derivate of this approach. Aristotle represents the western approach with the linear and logical philosophy. Galileo claimed that God speaks in the mathematical language. The Western approach is the "Masculine Principle" oriented, to which Jung attributed the concept: Masculinity = Animus. The Eastern approach is opposite: The world is perceived as a self-organized system, existing and terminated endlessly, without a creator, with no beginning and no end. Back in 1923 Jung (1963, Appendix 4) invited Richard Wilhelm to Zurich. Richard Wilhelm was the Marco Polo of the inner world of China. He is

DOI: 10.4324/9780429351518-18

responsible for opening up to the West the vast spiritual heritage of China, and thus all of Asia. He translated the great philosophical works from Chinese into German. Wilhelm validated to Jung "the other side" of the human psyche, the Anima. They became good friends. Jung realized the great significance of Wilhelm's work, especially the I Ching (based on the Ying and Yang - "Masculine" and "Feminine" traits). Jung helped Wilhelm gain respectability in the German academic community and wrote lengthy introductions to Wilhelm's two most important translations, I Ching: Book of Changes and The Secret of the Golden Flower. These two books had a profound influence on Carl Jung.

The idea of Anima (and Animus), which was first offered by Jung and further explained by his wife Emma Jung (1957), grants the Jungian coach a fantastic coaching tool to work with men, women, teams, and organizations. Stein (1998), in presenting the paradigm of Anima and Animus, brands them as "The Way to the Deep Interior" (103). In a simplistic way the idea of Anima and Animus proposes that in every human being (as well as in every organization) there are Feminine and Masculine qualities. In women there is an unconscious psychic Masculine entity called "Animus", and in men there is a corresponding unconscious psychic Feminine entity called "Anima". By the same token, both genders possess those two complementary traits to which we attribute the Feminine and Masculine Principles. Stein (1998) offers a condensed term for the two: Anima/us. Those two psychic entities are very important because Stein emphasizes that "the anima/us is an attitude that governs one's relationship to the inner world of the unconscious – imagination, subjective impressions, ideas, moods and emotions" (107). He continues: "Where there is anima/us, we want to go, we want to be a part of it, we want to join it, if we are not too timid or afraid of adventure" (117).

Consider this list of daily problems typical of corporate life: You must raise one million US dollars in order to promote a new initiative in your firm, and the time factor is critical. There is a problem with some suppliers who do not deliver the goods on time. The company's employees do not submit receipts and invoices on time. Too many workers are resigning from the company, and you find it hard to recruit talented personnel. You are responsible for booking complex flights for your company and your travel agent does not meet your expectations, but he is related to someone in the company's management. You are extremely ambitious, and you bring leads for potential clients to your company, but your managers do not establish good relationships with them and therefore your initiatives fail repeatedly. Although the team is very professional, it has serious problems with interpersonal relations, and you receive constant complaints about this. Your boss is acting aggressively toward you and even raises his or her voice sometimes. He or she is never satisfied. Dual management – in a matrix organization, your co-manager does not refer new workers to you for briefing and synchronization, or your co-manager holds an audit meeting without notifying you.

Has it ever occurred to you that all those problems and many more on a personal level can be dealt with, either from a Feminine or Masculine approach disregarding the client's gender? Responding from either the Feminine or Masculine principles will cause totally different results. Being able to choose and act from both principles grants the coachee an extended repertoire of responses with free choices in the deepest meaning of the word.

Stein (1998) *claims that* "the topic of defining Anima and Animus has become in many ways the most controversial, for it raises profound gender issues and suggests essential differences in the psychology of men and women" (104). For a reader who finds it irritating using Feminine and Masculine attributes I would offer a "circle" and "line" psychic database concepts, which represent two different opposing behavior sets which differ yet compliment each other. *Both genders can possess the "circle" and "line" traits.* The Anima/Feminine Principle stands for a "Being" approach and the Animus/Masculine Principle stands for a "Doing" approach to life. We shall discuss later in chapter 20 the immanent difference between the Feminine ("circle") vs. Masculine ("line") coping set of responses. We shall also examine which response would beneficially be recommended regarding the above list of dilemmas.

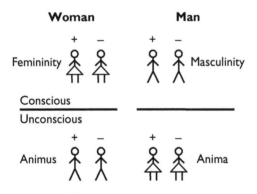

Figure 18.1 Four Options of Responses.

From a Jungian Coaching point of view, it would be advisable to always keep in mind *four options of responses* for both men or women facing life or professional challenges.

If the coachee is a woman – she may think, react, or process either from what we attribute as "positive Feminine" or "negative Feminine", or "positive Animus", or "negative Animus" modes of behaviors (chapter 14). If the coachee is a man, by the same token he may think, react, or process either from "positive Masculine" or "negative Masculine" or "positive Anima" or "negative Anima" modes of behaviors. We should strictly avoid judgmental attitudes while considering "negative and positive" aspects of an archetype. The "negative and positive" (same as in electricity) simply denote opposing traits on a longitudinal spectrum of traits that the archetypes hold. In coaching, as well as in life, there are times when what is considered "negative" is the very righteous or ethical act to perform or believe in. *The Jungian coach and coachee need to spot out which of the four options, the client pre-consciously responded from, versus which appropriate expected behavior best would have served the client in a challenging situation.*

Considering Femininity and Masculinity, Jung said that wholeness is the conjunction of you and me. By this he meant that any human who lacks relatedness to the other is lacking the wholeness, because the psyche cannot exist without its opposite side, which always dwells in the other. He also said that developing both our Feminine and Masculine sides has to do with Self-compensating our foundations. It happens through the completion of opposites and developing our inferior functions (Shadow!). This corresponds directly with the Flipping Principle (chapter 7), where the coach looks for the opposing compensating function, which will enable the coachee to balance his or her potentials.

There are many practical coaching insights (and techniques) for the immense Anima/Feminine principle, yet first one must understand *the origin of this concept, how it developed historically, and how it can be applied practically even nowadays on the individual and corporate coaching levels.*

To acquire the concept of Anima we need to consider six basic assumptions:

1. Anthropological decades of events, life traditions, and technologies shaped gradually the human consciousness and impacted its psyche (Harari, 2013, 2018).
2. Humanity, in prehistoric eras around 25000–6000 BC, psychologically speaking, was influenced and ruled by the Feminine, Nature, Matriarch Psychic Principle that dictated all human traditional life systems (Gimbutas, 2001 and Neumann, 1949, 1955).
3. There is a total difference between *Biological Gender* (Masculine and Feminine) and the *Psychological Database* to which we attribute, in Jungian psychology and coaching, the *"Masculine traits" (Animus)* and *"Feminine traits" (Anima)*. Both genders possess the whole spectrum of what is attributed psychologically to the Masculine and Feminine potentials. In both genders there are women with developed or undeveloped Femininity and developed or underdeveloped Masculinity (Animus). By the same token there are men with developed or underdeveloped Masculinity and developed or undeveloped Femininity (Anima).

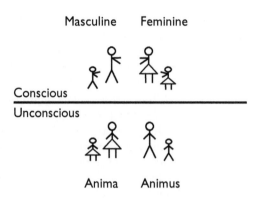

Figure 18.2 Developed and Underdeveloped Femininity/Anima and Masculinity/Animus.

Sexuality is common to both genders, and we should differentiate sexuality from the Feminine and Masculine principle.
4.   If we relate to a woman (by gender) we will relate to her Femininity and Animus, while in relation to a man (by gender) we shall relate to his Masculinity and Anima.
5.   Attributing certain traits to the Feminine and others to the Masculine (as is in the case of Ying and Yang) derives from human beings' psychic development as described by Neumann (1949). This delicate issue is discussed by Gary Toub (October 2013) in: Jung Page online educational resources for Jungian community, Jung Center of Houston.
6.   *Nature* is synonymous with the *Feminine* clustered traits (Bradley Zimmer, 1983).
7.   The Feminine and Masculine Principles are bipolar archetypes, and both have positive and negative traits (see Japanese fan, chapter 14).

What is the software of the Great Mother, the Feminine Principle, and the Anima (men's unconscious Feminine side). All three refer to the same psychological database. In "The Origin and History Source of Consciousness" (1949) and "The Great Mother" (1955), Neumann validates the historical roots of Jung's conception of the Anima and Animus. The Feminine Principle manifests itself through two polarities: On the *positive aspects* it is attributed Life, Nature, Fertility, Growth, Protection, Intuition, Containment, Patience, Circulation, Period, Emotions, Matter (ground, earthy), Nurturing, and Symbolization. Those positive traits are expected to naturally be developed throughout a woman's lifeline development, and if they are developed in a man as well, we shall claim that he has a *developed Anima*. On the *negative aspect* of the Feminine Principle we can identify the Instinct and Bestial Drives dictating motivation, Survival, and Creativity, which derive from everlasting change and breakdown of the known. *Example: A colony of ants is rushing away from great fire in the forest. They head instinctually toward a water obstacle, say, a river. About one-third commit suicide to instinctively create a floating bridge on which the rest will save the species. In corona pandemic we learnt the recent concept "Tribal vaccine" which refers to the same phenomena.*

Hysteria, Melancholy, Darkness, Captivity, and Lust are also variations of the negative side of the Feminine principle. Femininity is characterized by imagination under the obscure light of the moon (symbol of the Feminine). Circulation, or "circumambulate" is the characteristic Feminine line, meaning repetition and circularity way of movement or thought (opposing to the Masculine linear line and thought). It is manifested in nature in the biological phenomena of menstruation and the appearance and disappearance of the moon. Unconsciousness is the domain of the Feminine Principle. Transformation and development from one stage to another (as in Life) belong to the Feminine as well, where the cycle ends with Death and starts at Birth. Under the Feminine Principle survival is dedicated only for living and mating and is directed toward the searching for food. Surprisingly enough wars and human sacrifice are negative aspects of the Feminine instinctual drive for survival, as the *Matriarchal Principle does not acknowledge individuality and separation for it sanctifies the Collective.* Fascist regimes are based on the negative aspect of the Great Mother in the human psyche, where the individual is totally not important and is required to identify fanatically with the collective. A good example for the Feminine and Matriarch Principle and how a Masculine hero separates and individuates from the Matriarch is illustrated in Antz (1998), the computer animated adventure comedy film directed by Eric Darnell and Tim Johnson. In that movie we are accompanying a Hero/Ego character who is driven into an individuation process to risk himself out of a collective – negative – Feminine Matriarchal regime of the Great Mother colony under earth.

Chapter 19

The Animus/Masculinity archetype: Expanding toward outside

"I greet you, man on the high tower. I saw you from afar, looking and waiting. Your waiting has called me".

Red Book, Liber Secundus (pg. 259)

Of great contributions to the understanding of the Masculine archetype is Bolen's (1989) *Gods in Everyman*. Based on Greek mythology, through profound analysis of the Greek gods, Bolen teaches us the positive and negative qualities of the Patriarch, Masculine, or Animus psychology, which appeals to men and women's Masculine side. The theoretical and practical counterpart of the Anima archetype is the Animus, the Masculine unconscious database of women and the equivalent to men's conscious Masculine psychology. Neumann (1949) explains that from a psychic historical point of view the Masculine Principle emerged from the Feminine Matriarch only during the period of the Egyptian Pharaohs era. In accepting that the Masculine Principle derives from the Feminine principle, there lies a conclusion that essentially *the Feminine psychological principle is more sustainable than the Masculine principle. From a coaching point of view, in both the corporate and executive world and life coaching, this statement is crucial. It would mean that whenever an organization or an individual faces crises we should expect regressive response s, acts, and behaviors that are typical of the negative side of the Feminine Principle. Example: When Shiri Habib-Valdhorn of Globes, Israeli business arena newspaper, reported on 20 June 2019 that "after the Israeli company Teva fell again on Wall Street, rival generics pharmaceutical company Mylan now has a larger market cap than Teva", the practical indication of this title is mass dismissal. The HR department, had it been committed to the Masculine Principle, would have followed the principle that "last to come, first to go", yet, when the corporation struggles for its survival, very likely it adopts the negative side of the Feminine Principle, keeping the most valuable people and kicking out the vulnerable employees of Teva. However, Teva, in its good times, had a high reputation for its positive Femininity; nurturing its employees, granting them extended social conditions, and promoting the workers by expanding their assets.*

DOI: 10.4324/9780429351518-19

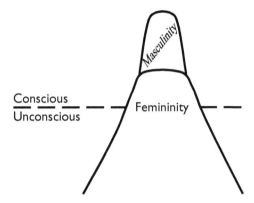

Figure 19.1 Masculine Derives from the Feminine.

For the reader to understand the Masculine Principle from a theoretical point of view, one needs to investigate the development and characteristics of the Patriarch Principle. What is the opposite of the Feminine Principle? What is the Patriarch, Masculine-Father Principle *in the human psyche*? According to Neumann (1955), the humans shift toward the Patriarchal Psychic stage is expressed in the myth of Isis and Osiris, the Egyptian gods. In the Matriarchal Egyptian society, young men were sacrificed on the altar of fertility and corps, fitting the negative side of the Matriarch-Feminine Principle. Out of the "collective emotion", in Egyptian mythology the image of the "Good God" named Osiris gradually developed (Larousse, 1959). "Osiris represents the corn, the vine and trees…the Nile which rises and falls each year" (p. 17). This description still keeps us under the positive aspect of the Feminine principle. Isis (a Greek rendering of Demeter), his sister, re-presents in the beginning the positive side of the Feminine principle as well: "she taught men the art of curing, instituting marriage and accustomed the Egyptians to domestic life". The Egyptian myth of Isis and Osiris, claims Neumann, conveys an *individual love* that reflects a shift toward the Masculine Principle. Larousse (1968) presents how those two god siblings Isis and Osiris fall in love, as Osiris was her eldest brother. "She was overwhelmed with grief at the news that Osiris had been assassinated by their brother, the violent Set who annihilated Osiris body into fourteen pisces which he scattered far and wide" (18). At this point the Egyptian mythology shifts to the Masculine principle, and into deep individual true love: "Isis, undiscouraged, searched for the precious fragments (of her brother Osiris) and found all except the phallus which had been greedily devoured by a Nile crab … the goddess reconstituted the body of Osiris".

The Patriarch culture is typical of rituals that signify the detachment from the symbolic womb symbolized by the Great Mother captivity (Matriarch regime). The purpose of all *Initiations Rituals* is to preserve and immunize the adolescent-individual from the negative side of Femininity: the destructive power of the unconscious is symbolized as grave, as a capturing uterus: the underworld, hell, destiny, or witch. In practical Jungian Coaching, initiation rituals can take place at the homework phase where the client commits to become proactive. Death, under the Patriarch, is conceived as eradication of the individual and its consciousness.

The idea of monotheism – Superior God in heaven and humans in his image – is in the Patriarch essence. Life is conceived rather differently than under the Feminine principle, as it is considered a superior value. Love is individual and relatedness stands beyond emotional collectivity. Individuality is conceived as a one entity and selfhood is praised. The Patriarchal society is a human society where its rules and characteristics derive from the Masculine side of the human psyche. The Patriarchal principle, on its positive side, includes logics, rationality, wording, and comprehending. Operating is based on principles, an abstract vision and the "word" has power and strength. Values, morality, rules, order, discipline, and hierarchy are characteristic of the Masculine domain. The "word" facilitates faculty of speech, conceptualization, and definition. Negotiation replaces war and power. The processes of enlightenment, light, and sun are the symbols of the patriarchal principle. Penetration transforms from the concrete (mating) to the abstract (intrusion to the depth of facts and meaning). If we summarized the main features that characterize the Masculine principle, we would count the linear line, speed, penetration-intrusion, rationale, mind, intellect, discipline, order, language, and individuality. Being an archetype, the Masculine principle has obviously a negative side as well: the dangers of religious fanaticism, physical aggression, hastiness, impetuous, structural rigidity, hierarchy, overspirituality, rationalizations, and politics.

E. Jung (1957) distinguished between four developmental stages of the Animus (and Masculinity): (1) the Masculine image of physical power; (2) the Masculine image which presents acts, authority, order, and organization; (3) the Masculine image presenting mind, analytic thinking, and words; and (4) the Masculine image of wisdom, spirituality, mysticism, values, meaning, and integration of the self. While Castillejo (1973), a Jungian analyst and great contributor for ethnic collective Feminine's wisdom, claimed that "the 'Positive Animus' functions as a lightened torch illuminating the woman's path, a guide who grants meaning and internal invisible support to a woman", Netzer (2019), disagrees with Castillejo. She believes Castillejo is wrong by attributing the Masculine principle (and men) as the psychic role model of self-guidance beyond any gender. Netzer (2019) proposes that "the "internal guide" is not the Masculine principle but rather the God Hermes, who is identified as the transcendent role player who arises the drive of Individuation" (p. 221). Netzer (2019) is preoccupied by the negative aspect of the Animus:

A woman can use the masculine principle by expressing opinions which seem truthful for her yet they are not authentically hers, she may find herself rigid, righteous, without awareness or self-criticism … she may develop guiding principle of intellectualism which is opposing her own psyche, which damages her Femininity and may cause neurosis. (p. 220)

Netzer (2019) counts four aspects of women attributions to the symbolic phallus in the last centuries: "curiosity, acknowledging their Shadow and owning it, cunning tricksterism and finally rage and aggression" (p. 244).

Greenfield (1983) specifies six phases of Masculine development (which count both to men and women's Animus): The Boy (called in Jungian terms "Puer Aeternus"=Eternal child), Don Juan, Trickster, Hero, Father and the Wise Old Man (Xenex).

In coaching we often meet clients with a discrepancy between their Persona (status, fame, role, reputation, occupation) and their level of Animus-development (in the case of women) or level of Masculinity (in a case of men).

Table 19.1 Greenfield's phases of masculinity-development and how they manifest in coaching challenges

	ANIMUS	MASCULINITY
Greenfield Phase of Masculinity	**When client is a woman**	**When client is a man**
Puer – Boy, Puella – Girl	Dependent on her parent or on her boss, ego-inflated with ideas without being able to actualize them, too enthusiastic, creative but childish and not productive. The coaching process needs to focus on "Pizza" proper functioning, the contract must be clear, and the client must learn to listen to her Self.	Dependent on a strong woman (Mom or patron), aerodynamic (moves a lot, changing jobs, locations, partners), sexually not developed; fascinates but does not develop relationships, creative but not productive. Coaching must focus on fulfilling precise assignments under the rule: make the less yet be authentic and show proven quality.
Don Juan	Seductive, men fall in her trap, she pulls them out of their comfort zone but does not create steady relationship, she uses her charms in business to promote herself, competes with the boss. She consumes coaching usually	Is driven to take the woman away from her "professional business, family's father". Breaks the rules and using his sex appeal. Skilled to make use of his handsome persona. He will consume coaching usually

(Continued)

Table 19.1 (Continued)

	ANIMUS	MASCULINITY
	because her "Don Juan/femme fatale" camouflage collapsed. Now it will be the time to gradually build up a Hero-Father Animus.	when he got mixed up with the law, blocked by bad reputation, is taken as unreliable. Coaching must be within a structured, target oriented contract, preferably coached by Animus developed female or authoritative male.
Trickster	Manipulative lady, politician, clever, and sharp, using contacts and her appearance (chapter 23). She will refer to coaching either because of chronic alteration of working places or defeat of her trickster maneuvers. Coaching must focus on reliability, authenticity, productivity, truthfulness. She needs to work intensively with her Shadow acknowledgment, accept, and face it. (chapter 21).	Politician, using his "metaphoric penis" to maneuver (chapter 23) (Pearlman, 2016, the psychopath executive). May use coaching as camouflage. Will consume coaching as a result of loss, defeat, or failure. Main challenge is to work with his shadow.
Hero	Determent, congruent, eager to move out of her comfort zone, she is target oriented (chapter 25). Will refer to coaching as part of her quest's advancement and will consider coaching as part of her road of trial. At times, because of over developed Animus, coaching will focus on developing her Femininity as a compensatory function.	Target and goal oriented, charismatic, leader (chapter 25). Usually the Masculine hero will refer to coaching as part of his internship on the road of trial. When the client is "anti-hero" but life forced him to take over the role of a hero, he will need leadership coaching (chapter 25).
Father	Very developed superego: ethical, respects the rules and law, good in expressing herself verbally and fond of language, scholar. She may refer to coaching because of too rigid and tough approach to life challenges or because of her inferior functions; undeveloped Femininity, too cognitive, too rigid or strict, paranoid of having issues in interrelationships.	A man of faith and trust, reliable, proven professional career, congruent, and respectful. His values are clear and linear. May refer to coaching because in his intimate life (family, family partners, life partners) he is emotionally reserved, competitive, punitive, or jealous. Additionally, he may

(Continued)

Table 19.1 (Continued)

	ANIMUS	MASCULINITY
		consume coaching to onset a second career.
Wise Old Man (xenex)	Experienced with life wisdom, depth, owns Feminine philosophy, trustworthy. May refer to coaching either because of loneliness or a wish to spread her wisdom lacking modern tools to market herself.	Mentor, honored member, member of board, owner of corporation or business before retirement, senior position. May refer to coaching in order to expand his point of view about matters, because of a need to fit in where age or tradition turn him irrelevant or not updated.

Chapter 20

Practical coaching with Anima and Animus

"Mother stone, I love you, I lie snuggle up against your warm body, your late child. Blessed be you, ancient mother".

Red Book, Liber Secundus (pg. 271)

The theoretical survey leaves us with a list of Feminine and Masculine databases, which, as coaches, can assist our clients. By applying them coachees can extend their behavior repertoires while facing problems in life. The assumption is that the more a person is accessing easily the *whole* spectrum of Feminine–Masculine responses (the Japanese fan), the more the person is competent, effective, and flexible in adjusting to challenges.

Let's get back then to the long list of problems issued in the beginning of chapter 18. In speaking about "Practical Anima and Animus", we assume that each of those problems maybe is raised in a coaching session by a different employee (a man or a woman) who claims he or she does not cope satisfactorily with the dilemma. As Jungian coaches we need to check three facts:

First, we need to evaluate the coachee's Masculine/Feminine level of development. Second we must cross compare this level with the client's Pizza–Ego functioning (Figure 12.1 in chapter 12). The Pizza itself has several categories that are more Doing/Masculine/Animus oriented (career, money, health/discipline, personal growth, spirituality) and several that are more Being/Feminine-/Anima- oriented (friends, family, intimate relationship, communal volunteering, nurturing physical environment).

Third, we need to define the "inferior function" of the client, meaning that side of the client's personality which appears "undeveloped" and needs to be brought up and practiced in coaching (chapters 21, 27).

In the Jungian Coaching method, we developed cards that allow the client to access their Anima/Animus/Masculinity/Femininity options of response. In the coaching session the coachee practices how to bring his or her adequate Anima/Animus repertoire into awareness.

To demonstrate this flow of coaching let us get back to the problems from the corporate life listed in chapter 18. One of the problems was: *There is a*

DOI: 10.4324/9780429351518-20

problem with some suppliers who do not deliver the goods on time. This problem can be approached from both Feminine and Masculine approach; obviously the results will be different.

If a client, facing this problem, is choosing the Feminine principle approach, he/she might pick up any of the "Pink Cards" (from the Feminie/Anima cards). The card may say*: Feel – what feelings come up in the presence of this problem – deal with them.*

If the client chooses to approach the problem from the Masculine Principle, he or she may use one of the "Blue Cards", and in that case the card may state: *This challenge that you are facing, what **Meaning** does it have in your career?.*

As instructed previously, the coach and coachee need first to find out which is the inferior function in the coachee's approach to the dilemma. If the instinctual approach is Feminine, then (by the compensatory function) the Masculine approach will direct the coachee to consider seriously what *meaning* those delays have on the coachee's career. This is a cognitive approach assuming that by understanding the meaning those delays have for the coachee, he or she might arrive at active conclusions which will lead to a new confronting attitude. However, if the person is cognitive, then a Feminine approach would be directed **inward**, leading to elaborate relevant *feelings* such as anger, frustration, and anxiety. Those feelings involved may cause the coachee to look at the delays symbolically and decide to take his or her emotional reactions as a practical sign.

Another problem: *You are extremely ambitious, and you bring leads for potential clients to your company, but your managers do not establish good relationships with them and therefore your initiatives fail repeatedly.*

Here too there are two modes of possible responses. Picking up randomly a Feminine principle card may challenge the client with this text: *By **Instinct**, don't think, what comes up on your mind?.* The Masculine principle card may offer randomly this text: *Use an existing **Hierarchy** in order to be assisted – consider seriously how to do it.*

If the coachee reacts too emotionally to this problem then the Masculine approach will suggest the coachee to consider how *hierarchy* is involved in dealing with that challenge and how to approach this hierarchy obstacle. Such approach might cause the coachee to confront and demand his mentor or CEO to re-evaluate the inter-relationships in the team. However, if the coachee is too rational, then the Feminine approach would direct toward possible *instinctual* solutions such as asking the coachee "think from your gut, what do you do in such a case?" This attitude may empower the coachee to be proactive and confront his team members by himself.

Last problem: *Although the team is very professional, it has serious problems with interpersonal relations, and you receive constant complaints about this.*

Once again the cards offer the client an option to respond to the challenge from those two styles, the Feminine and Masculine principles. The Feminine card, which was picked up randomly, said: *use your **Imagination** while thinking about this problem. What image do you see?*. The Masculine card, picked up randomly, may state: *Can you **Structure** the problem you face? use graphical charts.*

Masculine approach will offer ***structuring*** a workshop or set up regulations for better communication online or any planned intervention to improve communication, while the Feminine approach would suggest using the ***imagination*** to search for creative and irregular ideas.

Every life experience and problem solving can be responded to through either Feminine or Masculine Psychic modes. From a coaching point of view this is crucial as often our coachees react spontaneously either from a Feminine or Masculine positive or negative source, but their response is not necessarily adequate. Here are several examples where a man very likely will need to connect to his Anima in order to cope better in facing life or business challenges: Falling in Love and or other emotional responses a man feels will connect him to his Anima. If, unfortunately, a man's wife dies in an abrupt accident and he turns into a widower with three small children, he then would inevitably connect to his Anima. If a man was relocated and found his new boss a very tough, clever, intellectual, yet irrational, woman, he would better connect to his Anima. If a man reacts hysterically to stress at work, or, if in the midst of his career a man got a heart attack and things must slow down, or, if he is extremely gifted but has bad human relationships and no one wants to work with him, or if he is a troublemaker, or terribly competitive, in all those cases, inevitably he would end up dealing with his Anima repertoire. Those events may severely challenge a woman's Femininity as well if she is possessed by her Animus.

A good example of a young man with an undeveloped Anima who ends up changing his career in corporate life as his Anima increased by falling in love with his boss's daughter is *In Good Company*, a 2004 American comedy-drama film written and directed by Paul Weitz, and starring Dennis Quaid, Topher Grace, and Scarlett Johansson.

Jung (1982) explains brightly why it is difficult for a man to connect to his Anima:

> To anyone accustomed to proceed purely intellectually and rationally, this may seem altogether too ridiculous. It would indeed be the height of absurdity if a man tried to have a conversation with his Persona, which he recognized merely as a psychological means of relationship. But it is absurd only for the man who has Persona ... hence he is quite right to treat the Anima as an autonomous personality and to address personal questions to her. (p. 90)

Jung considers the "practical Anima" as a deep self-inquiry:

> Just as, for the purpose of individuation, or self-realization it is essential for a man to distinguish between what he is and how he appears to himself and to others, so it is also necessary for the same purpose that he should become conscious of his invisible system of relations to the unconscious, and especially of the Anima, so as to be able to distinguish himself from her. It is very difficult for a man to distinguish himself from his Anima, the more so because she is invisible. Indeed, he has first to contend with the prejudice that *everything coming from inside him springs from the truest depths of his being.* (p. 91)

The same counts for a woman who inevitably is required to face, develop, or acknowledge her Animus. There are a few movies circulating about this inevitable growth and empowerment. One prominent example is *Erin Brockovich*, a 2000 American biographical film directed by Steven Soderbergh, with Julia Roberts starring a character who fought against the energy corporation Pacific Gas and Electric Company.

If the Anima figure appears in coaching as a symbol for men, then Kast (1990) says, "we must be prepared to respond emotionally" (p. 15). Jung (1982) states that "The anima is a personality, and therefore she is so easily projected upon a woman. So long as the anima is unconscious, she is always projected, for everything unconscious is projected" (p. 86).

How does the Feminine Principle occur in women in coaching? Usually, in the postmodernist era, a woman, in the hi-tech, corporate, and business world, possesses a strong well-developed Animus. This sometimes might be on account of her spontaneous connectedness to her positive side of the Feminine principle. At times the overdeveloped Animus is an inborn talent. At other times it is developed through the compensatory function. Lack of a personal father, over identification with the father figure, local cultural values which praise the Masculine principle, or a result of trauma will reinforce a well developed Animus. At the same time, she might still be connected to the *negative side of the Feminine principle that seems to collaborate well with an inflated Animus.* When she presents problems and dilemmas in coaching, it would be advisable to practice the Feminine cards with her under the slogan "Retournons a la nature, Back to your Nature".

As both the Feminine and Masculine principles form a fan of multitude behaviors and values, it requires that the Jungian coach learn their manifestations. However, think about teamwork, couple, or family coaching – how helpful it is to sort out the Anima/Animus/Masculine/Feminine developmental level of each of the partners involved and how facilitating it would be both to bring their limitations to their awareness and practice with them the expansion of their "conscious gender" toward their "unconscious compensatory cross gender".

Regarding gay life, Hopcke (2007) contributes significantly to the analysis of Anima and Masculinity issues, challenging us by stating that:

> If the Anima can manifest itself in dreams in a form of an object or animal, why would she not appear in gay men's dreams in a form of a masculine figure. The essence of the Feminine archetype may in itself appear not feminine. While both men and women flow towards personal and collective androgynous psychic existence, would it be too exaggerating to find it on the archetypal level too. (p. 121, translated from Hebrew)

Both in the Hero Quest (chapter 25) and with the Leadership Archetypes (chapter 27), we shall notice the required Feminine and Masculine psychic traits.

Chapter 21

The Shadow archetype: The challenge of inferiority

"The image of God has a shadow. The supreme meaning is reals and casts a shadow".

Red Book, Liber Primus (pg. 230)

The Ego relates to Shadow as the Light to Shadow, says Jung; the bigger the light (person's activities), the bigger the shadowy pitfalls. This seems an interesting point inferring that there is no success without inevitable negative aspects accompanying it. Jungian Coaching, by principle, deals mostly with Shadow issues because finally people refer to coaching (in spite of their proven success), due to their failures, underprivileged conditions, their wish to change destiny, choices, ambivalence, fears, concerns, law self-esteem, and personal life curses. It is never too late to face and cope with one's own Shadow. It requires an optimistic, humble, humanistic, and courageous approach, but it will keep the client young, humble, creative, and a learning person. "By opening up to the shadow experience, a person becomes tainted with immorality but attains a greater degree of wholeness", says Stein (1998, 91), who also adds that "the shadow can be thought of as a subpersonality who wants what the persona will not allow" (90).

Here is a confession: I was born to become a therapist, teacher with natural talents, actor, musician, and artist. After 40 years of a vigorous psychotherapeutic career, I developed a clear and solid Persona: certified clinical and educational psychologist, Gestalt therapist, I submitted a doctoral dissertation in Self Psychology and Expressive Arts therapies, which led me to a tenure track position in the university. I developed a private clinic and intensive experience in public health services. Eventually, my profession led me to coaching in the business world, dealing with figures, contracts, commercial terms, and negotiations. Inevitably, I had to face my inferiorities; I was out of my comfort zone, falling into my Shadow, often referring to coaching, mentoring, and consultation. Although I own a whole list of credentials, still at the age of 67, I attend the CTI Israeli branch of

DOI: 10.4324/9780429351518-21

Co-Active Coaching training to become a certified coach, expand my Persona, and cope with my Shadow.

Baumann (2005), an Israeli Jungian analyst, writes:

> Knowing, means touching the unfamiliar – the dark – facing the psychic filth, the rage, ugliness, inferiority, deviation, obnoxious or anything perceived as dim or shady. One should remember that interacting with unconscious material evokes initially natural recoil which is followed by shame, guilt often defenses mechanisms, hiding away or projecting. (p. 21, translation from Hebrew)

My clinical career brought me to the conclusion that there are three sorts of Shadows (Goren-Bar, 2018, chap. 4): Human evil, Inferiority, and the White Shadow. Jungian Coaching focuses mostly on the last two. By identifying our client's weakness, by facing their inferiority, by acknowledging those drawbacks and offering our clients practical tools to deal with, we perform a "coaching Shadow work".

This is a legend I tell my students when approaching Shadow work: A man walks in the middle of the day, there's a sun in the sky, the man walks, and the long shadow follows him. The devil, wearing human clothes, crosses his path, enthusiastically points at the shadow and says: "Sell me your shadow!" The man turns around; he has not heeded that there was a shadow following him up to that moment. He thinks to himself: "I have managed so very well up until now without it, why should I keep it? He sold the shadow to the devil and died".

We deny our shadow and project it upon others. C.G. Jung said: The bigger the tree, the bigger the shadow!. Back in 1945 (after the Second World War), Jung gave a definition to the Shadow: "It is that thing which a human being would not wish himself to be". In that, he summarized the various sides and ways the Shadow can be expressed as the negative part in our personality. It is the sum of all the unpleasant parts of our personality that we would wish to hide away from, the inferior part in us, which is not worthy, the primitive part in human's character, the other person in us and the dark side of our personality. Jung emphasized in his writings once and again that we all possess a Shadow, that in the materialistic there's a shadow. Each one of us carries a shadow; however the less aware we are of our shadow, the less it is present in our consciousness. The less man knows about his shadow the darker and dangerous it is! If we are aware of our inferiority, we can repair it, even more; the shadow always creates coalition to other interests and always changes forms. *If it is denied, repressed, and isolated from our consciousness, it can never be controlled and might burst out and surprise us in moments of exhaustion or confusion. In any case it is an unconscious failure that ruins every good intention.* Coping with Shadowy challenges requires attention to instincts, to acts we do while losing our temper, being exhausted, short of money or assets, or being driven by an unrestricted drive.

The Shadow is an archetype, its form is universal, and all human beings possess the same forms of Shadow: the thief, the bandit, the violent character, the sexy woman, the rapper, the greedy, the ugly creature, the witch, the bad mother, the prisoner, the sadist, the image in black, the chaser, the crook, the intriguer, the macho, the whore – all are forms of our shadow.

As the shadow is an archetype, it always possesses immense power, operates strongly on the emotion, grasps us obsessively, controls us, it is autonomous and might overwhelm and deteriorate the personality. It has two sides: the negative (which we specified here), and the positive, the White Shadow. There are certainly inevitable moments, events, or acts in a human's life when immoral acts are done for the sake of moral motives. A starving refugee mother stealing food for her surviving children, a sexually abused employee charging her manager for harassment that eventually will ruin his life and family, a promoted employee who avoids telling her best friend at work (who competed with her) that she got the offer, hiding the news until it is officially announced.

Sophie's Choice, 1982, directed by Alan J. Pakula, is a good example of a white shadow, conveying Sophie (Meryl Streep), a Holocaust survivor, and how her life story (before, during, and after the war) compelled her to live white shadow relationships in order to survive; flashbacks reveal her harrowing story, from prewar prosperity to Auschwitz.

In Jungian Coaching the challenging issue of white shadow forces the coach and coachee into ethical dilemmas. As is for all contents which intrude our mind, in the beginning the shadow appears in a projective way: we are not aware of this negative trait in our personality that we deal with. Paradoxically, we identify that negative trait in our significant others: in my mother, my husband, a business partner, a miserable ugly child, my best friend, a member of the group, and our competitive partner or company. When we are aware of its prevalence in our personality, we sense anxiety and doubts. The shadow evokes powerfully and irrationally and is projected on the other for good (love) or for bad (hate)!

The first challenge is to identify the shadow image and find out how it manifests itself. Yet this is just the beginning of a shadow work. Control over the shadow is even tougher as one must relate to his or her Shadow with a strict educational manner, according to the principle: With it and against it! With it – as without it (according to the legend) one is not who he is. Against it – because when it dominates a person it destroys every good part and limits personal growth.

In the heart of the Jungian Coaching lies the work with the Shadow: A man with undeveloped Feminine traits (Anima), a woman whose scale of masculinity (Animus) traits is limited, or, conversely, a woman who is severely Animus-possessed, executives who got a promotion to a job which requires skills that are not in their arsenal, a person who suffers physical inferiority, a startup that runs out of budget or resources, a researcher who got poor results and is forced into restarting with a new method or technique, immigrants, refugees, and sickness – all are heroic states sentencing the Ego forces to step into a compulsory hero quest to face, own, and control over the Shadow. Coaching very often seems like a Shadow battlefield and Jungian Coaching offers tools to possess the Shadow and empower the challenged Ego.

Chapter 22

"Shadow work", an example

"Like plants, so men also grow, some in the light, others in the shadows. There are many who need the shadows and not the light".

Red Book, Liber Primus (pg. 230)

The shadow is not experienced directly by the Ego. Being unconscious, it is projected onto others. When one is tremendously irritated by a really egotistical person, for instance, that reaction is usually a signal that an unconscious shadow element is being projected.

(Stein, 1998, 88)

Here is an example for Working with the Shadow based on an attempt to control over projection.

1. **The Person, Issue, or Object Projected on...**
   Choose a person, an issue, or an object that bothers you continuously; address your complaints about him or her or it by writing one page of accusation!
2. **Aesthetic Distance**
   Go to an art buffett and create a sculpture that represents the person, object, or issue you projected your anger, resentfulness, or hate on.

DOI: 10.4324/9780429351518-22

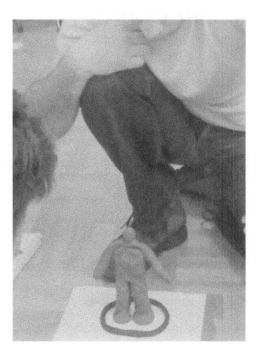

Figure 22.1 Working with the Shadow.

3. **The Dialogue**

Create a dialogue with the sculpture you have just created (your Shadow object).

One side is You – other side is the autonomous sculpture talking. Make this dialogue at least five times!

You: ....

Sculpture/Shadow: ....

You: ....

Sculpture/Shadow: ....

You: ....

Sculpture/Shadow: ....

You: ....

Sculpture/Shadow: ....

You: ....

Sculpture/Shadow: ....

4. **Internal lesson**

Say out loud: This _____ (give it a name, either the person's name, or the dilemma's name or the object's name) came into my life to teach me an important lesson. The lesson must not deal with the real person, dilemma, or object but rather it is How Do You intend to deal with Yourself in the presence of this person, dilemma, or object. Find the name of the lesson: _____.

5. **Contract**

Write a one-page contract specifying how you will educate yourself on how to contain, tolerate, put borders on, ignore, or deal with the lesson you took upon yourself as a result of the present you were given by the "Projected Figure".

6. **Letter of gratitude**

6a Sit in front of your sculpture and hold it or touch it with both your hands. Tell your sculpture YOU are grateful it came to your life. Explain in detail how this challenge will make you a better person.

6b Sit with yourSelf and write a half page letter of gratitude to your Shadow Figure:

Dear _____...

Chapter 23

The Trickster archetype: About politics and manipulations

"I must also speak of the ridiculous. You will recognize the supreme meaning by the fact that he is laughter and worship, a bloody laughter worship".

Red Book, Liber Primus (pg. 230)

In Jungian Coaching we consider the Trickster archetype as a potential change locomotive required for the coachee to connect with in order to move forwards.

The Trickster Archetype is affiliated to the Shadow and the negative side of the Anima/Femininity Principle. Jung (1969) points out how the Anima connects to the Trickster. Do remember we do not speak here about a woman by gender but rather about the negative psychic archetype of Femininity and how it affiliates to the Shadow. Jung writes: "the one standing closest behind the shadow is the Anima, who is endowed with considerable powers of *fascination and possession*. She often appears in rather too youthful form and hides in her turn the powerful archetype of the wise old man" (p. 150). By this Jung meant that one way of manipulating derives from an attractive behavior that uses charms, sex appeal, or emotional talents to fascinate people (see chapter 19). The Trickster archetype is unfortunately quite popular in corporate life. Pearlman (2016) claims that:

> About one in five corporate executives are psychopaths – roughly the same rate as among prisoners. The study of 261 senior professionals in the United States found that 21% had clinically significant levels of psychopathic traits. The rate of psychopathy in the general population is about one in a hundred.

Nathan Brooks, a forensic psychologist who conducted the study, said the findings suggested that businesses should improve their recruitment screening. He said recruiters tend to focus on skills rather than personality features, and

DOI: 10.4324/9780429351518-23

this has led to firms hiring "successful psychopaths" who may engage in unethical and illegal practices or have a toxic impact on colleagues. "Typically, psychopaths create a lot of chaos and generally tend to play people off against each other," he said. Whether this report is reliable or not, it corresponds to what Jung described first back in 1969. Jung argues that "The so-called civilized man has forgotten the trickster ... he never suspects that his own hidden and apparently harmless shadow has qualities whose dangerousness exceeds his wildest dreams" (p. 147). The Trickster archetype says Jung is "a suitable designation for this character component when I call it shadow ... are the defects of the conscious personality ... there are remnants of a collective shadow figure which prove that the personal shadow is in part descended from numinous collective figure" (p. 142). He goes on claiming that:

> The peculiar thing about these dissociations is that the split-off personality is not just a random one but stands in complementary or compensatory relationships to the ego-personality. It is a personification of traits of character which are sometimes worse and sometimes better than those the ego-personality possesses. (p. 142)

Here Jung points out that certain aspects of the Trickster archetype are beneficial and practical in addition to the coachee's personality.

> Only when his consciousness reached a higher level could he (the trickster personality) detached the earlier state from himself and objectify it, that is, say anything about it. So long as his consciousness was itself trickster-like, such confrontation could obviously not take place. It was possible only when the attainment of a newer and higher level of consciousness enabled him to look back on a lower and inferior state. (p. 143)

This means that we should differentiate between a coachee who acts from a Trickster approach without being aware of his or her manipulative behavior and a coachee who needs to adapt Trickster traits to be able to manage better in his or her daily assignments.

Many movies display tricksters in corporate life; however, I found *The Devil's Advocate*, a 1997 American supernatural horror film directed by Taylor Hackford and starring Keanu Reeves and Al Pacino, a good example for sophisticated trickster in the business world. Pacino's character, Satan, takes the guise of a human lawyer. Jung describes the Trickster's traits (while reading think about executives and other professionals you may know): "He (or she) is a forerunner of a savior, and like him (or her), God, man and animal at once. He (or she) is both subhuman and superhuman, a bestial and divine being, whose chief and most alarming characteristic is his (or her) unconsciousness. Because of this he (or she) is deserted by his/her companions, which seems to indicate that he/she has fallen below their level of consciousness. He (or she) is so unconscious of himself/herself that his/her body is a reference of their original nature as a Creator ... is not a unity, and his/her two hands fight each other ... even his or her sex is optional despite its phallic qualities; he/she can turn himself/herself into a woman or man) and bear children. From his or her metaphoric penis he/she makes all kinds of useful plants" (p. 146).

How does the Trickster archetype appear in Jungian Coaching and when is it possible to recruit this psychic "talent" in the process of personal growth? Jung (1969) claims that "typical trickster motifs can be found in the alchemical figure of Mercurius. His powers as shape-shifter, his dual nature, half animal, half divine ... his approximation to the figure of a savior" (p. 135). Those personality qualities are essential first for any individuation process when one wishes to depart from the comfort zone. There are inevitable trickster-acts that one must manipulate and execute in order to gain freedom, opinion, liberty, or flexibility in life. I have been coaching people who looked for a release from a strict "Father" ruler or from a "negative Feminine captivity" (those can include family suppression, boss abuse, law self-esteem oppression, and fears of tradition and religiosity). *Only connectedness with the unconscious Trickster's qualities can help the coachee free himself or herself.* Dialoguing with the internal archetypal image of the Trickster is a very dramatic expereince with a psychic impact of initiation. In managerial proactive positions, under corporate competitive culture and in the face of excellency as top value, the only approach advisable to survive is to connect with the Trickster qualities database.

TRICKSTER

Archetype symbolizing the
instinctual, manipulative,
artistic, clever and political side
in a human being. Essential for
mediation.

©AviGorenBar

Figure 23.1 The Trickster Coaching Card.

Figure 23.2 The Trickster.

When relating to the women's Trickster archetype we should consider C. Nagel (2020), who states that "we live in a world where gender biases and stereotypes prevail in the corporate environment" (p. 124). Tannen (2007) contributes to the understanding of the Trickster phenomena through the Feminine gender. Following Kast (1993), Tannen asks: "How does the imagination produce new metaphoric imagery which if grasped, *has the potential to trick and transform?*" (p. 60). She leans on the Trickster archetype to free the woman: "Trickster appears to model change and possibilities" (p. 7). She argues, "The single most significant aspect of the postmodern female trickster is the integral role that social work plays in their behavior. This is the part of the transformed ethical orientation in the postmodern female Trickster which results in the construction of an identity which refuses to be victim" (p. 9) and by using the Animus trying to free the woman from the Patriarch suppressive attitude. Tannen and Netzer (2019) add the Trickster archetype to the female Jungian Coaching toolbox. Tannen concludes: "Humor is the energy, movement is the process and embodiment is in a female image who refuses to be a victim of the collective consciousness which restricts feminine energies manifesting psychological authority, bodily autonomy and physical agency" (p. 10). When Netzer (2019) surveys the notion of the female's phallus, she specifies "cunning" as one of its prominent traits: "The demand for total obedience from the female blocks her development". Netzer quotes Campbell (1998, p. 73), stating that "real life began with disobedience!". Cunning is an important shadow trait alongside the Hero Quest and corresponds with the Animus. It enables the heroine to operate in the world while bypassing chanceless direct confrontation in the suppressing Patriarch. This means that a woman in a coaching context, who wishes to free herself from possessing authority, limitations or restrictions, must inevitably connect to the Trickster archetype. The "Tricksteress' arsenal includes manipulation, concealment, lies, stilling, sophistry, impersonation, those are the fighting tools of the weak but of women as well" (p. 235). The Feminine trickster, Netzer clarifies, "has sexual, passionate and Trickster qualities" (p. 238). In practical coaching if a woman is in the individuation process, we should connect her to her Ego, Animus, and Trickster qualities, while if a man is in coaching, his trickster, as Jung claimed, will hide in and under his Anima, using his Persona to maneuver people. A good example of a woman trickster is played by Meryl Streep again, this time in *The Laundromat*, 2019, directed by Steven Soderbergh. Ellen Martin, a post-traumatic widow, begins investigating a fake insurance policy by using inevitably trickster repertoire when her idyllic vacation takes an unthinkable turn.

Chapter 24

A Jungian Coaching approach to money issues

"Pleasure immediately attracts everything you desire, and then you must decide whether your pleasure spoils or enhances you".

Red Book, Liber Primus (pg. 263)

In this chapter we would like to use a symbolic thought to decipher the essence of all businesses - Money. What does it stand for and what hides behind it psychologically. We would also examine the Jungian Coaching approach to money issue.

As an extension to the Trickster archetype is Netzer's (2008) interesting Jungian point of view on the psychology of money. A positive aspect of the Trickster archetype relates to money and money making. Paradoxically, opposing money considerations is the Fool archetype, which presents a variation on the Trickster theme. The Fool ignores all materialistic considerations and is presented as the Shadow side of Hermes the god of merchants and Thieves. The Fool (p. 42) is shown at the beginning of his journey with unlimited potential.

We have here an X-ray picture of the enthusiastic start-up entrepreneur who is highly motivated and looks at the future with visions that at times are far beyond the perception of his colleagues or family:

The sun, rising up behind him, represents the beginning of his journey. He is facing north-west, the direction of the unknown (America?). He is looking upwards, toward the sky, or spirit. He is about to step off a cliff into the material world but is he prepared? He has all the tools and resources he needs in the bag on his staff, but he has not opened the bag yet. The white rose in his left hand represents purity and innocence. (Netzer, 2008)

This description reminds us of the *Crossing of the Threshold in the Hero Quest* (chapter 25).

DOI: 10.4324/9780429351518-24

Figure 24.1 The Fool.

He has a guardian in the form of a little white dog who will protect him throughout his journey but who will also push him to learn the lessons the fool came here to learn. The dog represents the instincts which are preliminary assets for every entrepreneur. The mountains behind the fool represent the realms of spirit that he has just left and will spend his life trying to regain. (p. 44). By now, we have encountered , as Jungian Coaches, several tools to coach a client who represents the Fool. The Macilune cards (corresponding to the Kagulatio Alchemical technique) will focus the Fool on practical achievements. The Feminine cards (corresponding to the Solutio Alchemical technique) will expose the emotional aspects of the Fool's motivation.

Now let's get hold of the coin. A client is involved in or tangled with financial matters. As Jungian coaches, reading the symbolic monologue of the coin, presented by Netzer (2008), we are granted a list of practical considerations to apply in coaching. We are expected to translate the symbolic knowledge given to us here, into practical acts.

Netzer (2008) clarifies that: "The money (the physical object) is symbolized by the Pentagram which speaks for itself:" *Me, the Circle, inside me the Pentagram, starts with five points. I am the Pentateuch. Earth foundation. I am sensation, the senses that grant odor and taste for all pleasures. I am the materialistic, the earthy, the concrete, the substantial, the one who grants*

Figure 24.2 Pentagram.

security and a basis for reconsiderations. I am the physical body foundation, reality, concrete and rational." First while coaching clients with financial issues we need to adopt a conscious, earthy, practical attitude toward the dilemmas the coachee brings up.

"I am the coin, the current money, the economic consideration and worthiness of life. I am the coin which influences human traits and human's attitude towards himself and others, as a man is judged upon his pocket. I reinforce competition, achievements, generosity, thriftiness, as well as greediness, wastefulness, miserliness, jealousy, quackery and burglary." Here we face the Shadow side of the financial interactions.

"I am the pentagram locked in a closed frame which acknowledges the limitations of reality and human beings. The form that acknowledges health, property, interest, practical thinking, importance of work, efforts, training, suspension of gratification, self-discipline, commitment, and responsibility. All these enable boundaries, limits, focusing, organizing, and programming human operations in this world at family and social systems." This list relates to the Masculine traits of the financial considerations, mainly Ego functions.

"I am the ground pentagram that balances the wind's flight, so I enable taking off feelings, intuition, and vision with the intention to return and enrich the earth. Also, I am the golden pentagram, symbolizing spiritual values, balance and possible mental wholeness, which turns the materialistic into spirituality, finds increased value meanings like the divine sparkling within the

physical universe." This aspect of money issues illuminates the compensatory spiritual side of the financial business.

"*My limitation is a narrow point of view on the world through the hole of the penny, calculations of exaggerated cost, considering only the economic value and stinginess. Or, the opposite: relating solely to spirituality ignoring and denying the materialistic*"(p. 113). Here again the coin points out at another Shadowy aspect of a financial involvement.

Chapter 25

The Hero Quest – coping with postmodern career

"Letting things happen, the action through none-action, the 'letting go of yourself', became the key for me that succeeded in opening the door to the way; One must be able to physically let things happen".

Red Book, Liber Primus (pg. 237)

The hero archetype and the hero quest offer Jungian Coaching a great tool in coaching issues that deal with process, career, self-development, and growth. Whenever the coachee's topic has "a before and after" aspect, the Jungian Coach should consider the option to practice the Hero coaching tool.

The ancient Greeks in mythology saw "Heroism" a central theme because it corresponded to "'Fate" (a predetermined course of events). If you are born with a fate, what is the point to expect anything from life, your fate will dictate it anyway. Well, this is the insight we learn from the ancient Greeks: If you fight your fate you become a Hero and you curve your own "Destiny". Fate and destiny are both words dealing with a predetermined or destined future. However, while fate is concrete and determined by the cosmos, destiny depends on your choices in life, your potential heroism.

The Jungians took this concept – fighting the impossible – and turned it into an archetypal quest. M. Stein (1998) says that Jung "outlined the constellation of the hero myth and assigned to *the hero the role of creating consciousness*" (75). This means that by struggling, investing efforts, and stepping out of the comfort zone, one ascends his or her awareness and realizes its own qualities. Stein (1998) refers here to the tremendous challenge in assimilating unconscious ideas and irrational situations to daily ego-consciousness reality. This assignment is heroic from the Jungian point of view. The psychic mission to connect the ego (the coachee) to his or her unconscious and work on the Ego-Self axis is challenging and considered by the Jungians as a "Hero Quest". Samuels (1985) quotes Neumann (1955, pp. 114–115), who stated: "Making these differentiations (between

DOI: 10.4324/9780429351518-25

consciousness and unconscious) is a heroic act" (p. 71). What are those differentiations? It is expected from a person to be able to heed to his or her unconscious ideas, thoughts, desires, fears, and concerns and find appropriate means to actualize and incorporate those into daily life in such a way that they fit, contribute, and push forward life's development. There is a misleading factor in this daily phenomenon; people normally attribute external events or conditions to their life choices, decisions, and acts as they believe they mostly respond out of an adaptation to reality. A Hero (in the Jungian sense) is the one who responds to his or her inward awareness. When God commanded Abraham to leave his birth homeland to the place where he'd lead him, tempting him with the promise to turn his sperm into people big as much as the sea sand, he challenged Abraham to become a hero and follow an internal belief, as he didn't mention a specific destination, just said: "to the place where i'd lead you". Neumann explains three psychological goals (stages) which the hero tries to achieve in his struggling quest:

> First, the hero/ego is trying to separate from the mother and the maternal environment (in Jungian coaching terms this means the coachee needs to move out of his comfort zone = habits, routine, the known and familiar). Second, the hero is trying to identify and discriminate the Masculine and Feminine sides of himself, so as to integrate them (in Jungian coaching this means, in a man's case, a serious attempt to assess the level of his Masculinity's functioning and the ability to connect to his Anima. In a woman's case to estimate her Femininity's functioning and balance it with a developed Animus). Third, he is looking for values and modes of psychological functioning to offset and balance the over-directed and exaggeratedly conscious manner he has had to develop to break out of the embrace of the Great Mother (in Jungian coaching this means arrive to an integrated personality which benefits the whole spectrum of Masculine and Feminine potential). (Samuels, 1985, p. 71)

In all cultures throughout history, human beings connected, created, and praised the archetypal image and legends of the Hero Quest. Campbell (1988) suggested a 17-stage paradigm – found in most mythologies – which includes three phases in the common Hero journey: The departure, The road of trials, and The return. In all those 17 stages the crucial point is how – in the presence of challenges – the Hero heeds inwardly and in response acts outward. In the Jungian Coaching method, we adopted 15 of those steps to characterize the quest of an employee's career in the postmodern corporate world.

Figure 25.1 Hero Quest.

Apparently, those steps fit properly to every life stage a person goes through. Same person can be situated in his or her lives at different stages, on different problems along the Hero Quest *(Example: One may be deep in "the road of trials" in his/her business life yet terribly stuck in "the belly of the whale" in marriage)*.

The Jungian Hero Quest coaching method is based on *two levels:* First, the coach, through the hero quest cards, increases the clients' emotional, cognitive, and physical awareness. Second, the coach creates a mini laboratory for change to practice (in simulative conditions) the innovative behavior the coachee is expected to adopt while fitting a particular stage in the hero quest. In the Jungian Coaching method, we put emphasis on *three aspects* for each stage on the Hero Quest; the *benefit* the coachee can make out of that particular stage, the inevitable *price* he or she will apparently pay, and, most important, the *insight* one can gain while lodging in that stage. We developed three experiential cards for each of the 15 stages.

We will approach the Hero Quest concept in Jungian Coaching when a client is intrigued with a business, professional, or life dilemmas that involve a process. Obviously the coachee and coach are required to properly fit the case brought up in the session to the appropriate stage on the Hero Quest. Each of the cards (benefit, price, and insight) presents three existential states; cognitive, emotional, and physical (as we believe every stage on the Hero Quest grasps the person in a holistic manner). The coachee chooses one of the three options (benefit, price, or insight) and on that option he or she is invited to choose to experience, in the here and now, one of those three existential states (thinking, feeling, or sensing). The Diamond (benefit) Card – is advised to be picked up and experienced first, when the coachee needs to be encouraged. The Sword (price) Card – when the coachee needs to be discouraged as he or she is too motivated and the Owl (insight) Card when an insight is required in considering a crucial step.

Here are the 15 steps we apply in coaching the Hero Quest:

First Phase: *Departure.*

Stage one: *The Call for Departure.* The hero starts off in an everyday situation of normality from which some information is received that acts as a call to head off into the unknown. In coaching, such situations are typical for relocation, if the client was dismissed, or if he comes up with a vision, dream, or a new idea. Also, if the client complains about boredom, or was offered a promotion.

This first stage (*call for adventure*) is instinctual due to its spontaneity and functions as a *drive*, therefore it may be considered as belonging to the Feminine principle. Here are examples of the text which the client is advised to experience if he or she was found located in the stage 1: departure.

THE CALL TO ADVENTURE (SWORD)
1 DEPARTURE

1. *I am the inevitable fear attacking you. Where am I located in your body? How do I look and what do I say to you?*
2. *I am the depressive and bored feelings which prevent you from going happily to work.*
3. *I am the new role you have just obtained from your boss.*

THE CALL TO ADVENTURE (DIAMOND)
1 DEPARTURE

1. *I am the dream telling you about the big change to occur in your life.*
2. *I am the burden and depression from where you need to emerge into new life.*
3. *I am the new position you just received.*

THE CALL TO ADVENTURE (OWL)
1 DEPARTURE

1. *I am the awareness of your internal irrational voice which pushes you to change something in your career.*
2. *I am your drive for adventure, risk taking, persistency, and devotion.*
3. *I am your right to give yourself what you need in the most egocentric sense.*

Stage Two: *Refusal of the Call.* Often when the call is given, the future hero first refuses to accept it. This may be from a sense of duty or obligation, fear, insecurity, a sense of inadequacy, or any of a range of reasons that work to hold the person in his or her current circumstances. It is expected in coaching to contain and elaborate the clients' concerns: fear, psychosomatics, constraint, budget issues, and family. This second stage has to do with reconsiderations, evaluations, and perspective; therefore, it may be attributed to the Masculine principle. In addition to the cards of this stage, the long list of Masculinity traits is recommended to be considered for coaching (chapter 19) as they will help the client move on towards the next stage in life.

Stage Three: *Supernatural Aid.* Once the hero has committed to the quest, consciously or unconsciously, his guide and magical helper appears, or becomes known. Often, this supernatural mentor will present the hero with one or more talismans or artifacts that will aid them later in their quest. This stage presents the coachee's motivation to refer to coaching or therapy, to appeal for a grant, seek knowledge and search for support. Think of Columbus, at this stage, inevitably spending precious time, knocking on kings' doors to obtain support, having in mind the notion of an expedition to cross the Atlantic. This stage may be considered a Feminine principle stance as the hero withstands seeking for nurturing assets.

Stage Four: *The Crossing of the First Threshold.* This is the point where the person crosses into the field of adventure, leaving the known limits of his world and risking into an unknown and dangerous place where the rules and limits are not known. In coaching we accompany the coachee with traveling issues, reorganizing life as a passage, preparing the client to interview or exams, embarrassing the client through a disease (possible psychosomatic regression before change), or accepting a verdict. From the Feminine/Masculine principles point of view here is a paradox; although at this stage the client may need nurturing support, at the end of the day, he must perform an abrupt move – a Feminine impulse – to eventually step out from the comfort zone. Indeed, the next step will lead the coachee into the second phase of the Hero Quest.

Stage Five: *The Belly of the Whale*. This stage represents the final separation from the hero's known world and self. By entering this stage, the person shows willingness to undergo a metamorphosis. This stage is impressive from a coaching point of view. The belly of the whale paradoxically invites the coachee, not without suffering (chapter 16) to integrate himself, build up a cohesive Self, and check the level of motivation for the quest one last time. Usually people who refer to coaching expect in a short coaching process to be pulled out from dead ends as soon as possible. Here, the Jungian approach, just like Zen Buddhism, Hassidic, Sufi, and ancient wisdom, is urging the coachee to surrender to the solitude this stage offers and make the best out of this inevitable halt. Furthermore, in accordance with the coaching ethics, it is the coachee who eventually helps himself out of this stage, while the coach is out there holding hope for his client (chapter 11). Just like the frog who shakes the milk with its fins, turning it into cheese and jumps out of the milk's barrel, so does the coachee, eventually finding out the rationale for being stuck. Therefore, Jungian Coaching embraces situations such as temporary depression or mood, state of stuck, delay, surgery, expectations, no promotion, not knowing, and ambivalence, and approaches those states as existential lessons for life. Here the coach is expected to help the coachee make out the meaning of this stage. Obviously, this incubation stage is Feminine principle–oriented.

Second phase: *The Initiation.*

Stage Six: *The Road of Trials*. The road of trials is a series of tests, tasks, or sufferings that the person must undergo to begin the transformation. Often the person fails one or more of these tests, which often occur in threes. This stage is the daily bread of every coach and it includes practical challenges, and issues such as jobs, projects, competition, sufferings, and obstacles that the coachee brings along to the coaching process. It is Masculine principle–oriented as it is usually a linear, target-oriented process that has to do with "doing" achievement tasks.

Stage Seven: *The Meeting with the Goddess*. In this stage Campbell adopted the psychodynamic attachment theory of the baby to the maternal image. This is the point when the person experiences a love that has the power and significance of the all-powerful, total surrender, unconditional love that a fortunate infant may experience with his or her mother. This is a very important step in the quest and is often represented by the person finding the other person that he or she loves most completely (explains why people fall in love at work). People may arrive at coaching in this stage because their "Ego Pizza", in the career/ working category is inflated. Workaholism, success, devotion, and total commitment to work on account of personal life have become their priority. Usually at this stage coaching will focus on Shadow issues, and balancing the client's preferences and activities will be centering on the compensatory function (chapter 6). This stage is characterized by the negative side of the Feminine principle (seduction, enrapture).

As in all stages, here too we will demonstrate a three-card example that the client is offered to experience at this stage:

THE MEETING OF THE GODDESS (SWORD)
7 INITIATION

1. *I am the feeling of dependency and the insight that you will always need somebody to be happy.*
2. *I am this sexual desire which weakens you and causes you addiction and dependency.*
3. *I am your workaholism.*

THE MEETING OF THE GODDESS (DIAMOND)
7 INITIATION

1. *I am that physical pleasure arising in the encounter between two harmonious beautiful bodies.*
2. *I am that wonderful feeling of "better the two than the one".*
3. *I am the devotion and love towards your quest's goal.*

THE MEETING OF THE GODDESS (OWL)
7 INITIATION

1. *I am this insight that although I can do alone I simply prefer partnership.*

2.   *I am the insight about:"A healthy soul is in a healthy body!"*.
3.   *I am this insight that every Hero needs a warm and comforting place to refuel.*

Stage Eight: *Woman as a Seduction*. As an extension of the previous stage, this obsession and attachment to the job is symbolized by the negative side of the Feminine Principle. We may interpret symbolically this stage as falling into an inevitable Shadow. In this step, the hero faces those temptations that may lead him or her to abandon or lose his or her quest, which does not necessarily have to be represented by a woman. Here again the woman is solely a metaphor for the physical or material temptations of life, since historically the hero-knight was often caught by lust in his spiritual journey.

There are three categories of Shadow here: financial, sexual, and power. From coaching point of view this stage is challenging the coach because inevitably the coach needs to deal with ethical issues as the coaching alliance might be tested by contents of corruption, sex, drug addiction, and aggression.

Stage Nine: *Regret Assisted by the Father*. Once the hero makes a success often, irresistibly, he or she falls into his or her own shadow. This step is associated with corruption, ethics, and government capital issues. The Father Archetype can alleviate him (or her Animus in a woman's case). In this step the person must confront and be forgiven by whatever holds the ultimate power in his or her life. In many myths and stories this is the father, or a father figure who has life and death power. This is the center point of the journey. All the previous steps have been moving into this place, all that follow will move out from it. Although this step is most frequently symbolized by an encounter with a male entity, it does not have to be a male; just someone or something with incredible power. In coaching we need to deal here with the law and discipline (contract between the coach-coachee, punctuality, payment, and commitment). Occasionally a rehabilitation or schooling program is required. This stage is characterized by the Masculine principle.

Stage Ten: *Apotheosis (Total Nirvana)*. Accepting and committing to the "Father principle" balances the hero and approximates him or her to a mature chapter in his career. Start-up and hitch employees target toward achieving this dream. The coachee has gained the certificates required; he might have obtained honored citizenship, publication, and fame, and by now can live in spirit. He moves beyond the pairs of opposites to a state of divine knowledge, love, compassion, and bliss. This is the Cinderella or Superman desired status. A simpler way of looking at this step is that it is a period of rest, peace, and fulfillment before the hero begins an optional return. People refer to coaching at this stage when they consider a second career (sometimes as they have made their "exit", other times as transformation). Contents such as self-containment (mindfulness), hobby, vacation, voluntary work, spiritual activity, or education are dealt with during coaching. This stage is a balance between the Feminine and Masculine principles.

Third Phase: *The Return.*

Stage Eleven: *Refusal of the Return.* Having found bliss and enlightenment in "the other world", the hero may not want to return to the ordinary world to share his or her success with others. This stage resembles stage two, *Refusal of the Call.* When a successful person needs to "return" (relocate back to his or her homeland, bequeath a successful business to his or her descendants, submitting knowledge he or she gained throughout his or her life, give up on power and wealth because of illness, age, values) he or she may refer to coaching. In coaching it is expected to deal with the client's shadow on issues such as egocentric considerations, stinginess, control, and puritan attitudes. Here a dialogue on the Ego-Self Axis is advisable (chapter 15). The cards offered the coachee to experience on this stage are brought here as an example:

REFUSAL TO RETURN (SWORD)
11 THE RETURN

1. *I am this immense suffering on giving up everything I have achieved in order to return to where I had come from.*
2. *I am the uncertainty to succeed in the original place where I came from, as I did here.*
3. *I am the difficulty to give up on the gratifying habits I have become accustomed to here and return to my original place.*

REFUSAL TO RETURN (DIMOND)
11 THE RETURN

1. *I am the ability to pass over the knowledge and values gained throughout my quest.*
2. *I am the ability to sustain the return, so that I can rest before returning.*
3. *I am the wish to hold back the knowledge acquired in the quest and keep it for myself.*

REFUSAL TO RETURN (OWL)
11 THE RETURN

1. *I am the insight that spreading around my knowledge is my life quest.*
2. *I am the insight that I need to build my own successors.*
3. *I am the insight that the direction of my career led me finally to where I had started.*

Stage twelve: *The Magic Flight.* Sometimes the hero must escape with his or her achievements, if it is something that the gods have been jealously guarding (meaning it has valuable importance to either the consumers or the local regime). It can be just as adventurous and dangerous returning from the journey as it was to go on it. In the corporate world such cases are known as headhunting, discreetly attending interviews to upgrade positions, downsizing and merging, gaining knowledge with an attempt to establish later a competitive endeavor, moving technology elsewhere, forwarding fortune or business from one country to another. This stage requires certain trickster talents from the coachee (chapter 23) and they correlate to the negative side of the Feminine principle (instinct and survival). However, there is a positive side to this stage as well when the coachee wishes to invest his or her assets in a discreet manner; anonymous donation, scholarships, and voluntary work.

Stage thirteen: *Rescue from Without.* Just as the hero may need guides and assistants to set out on the quest (stage three), oftentimes he or she must have powerful guides and rescuers to bring them back to everyday life, especially if the person has been wounded or weakened by the experience. In the coaching process, issues such as partnership, downsizing, retirement and pension, legacy, and heritance are brought up. This stage is characterized by the Masculine principle as it has to do with collaboration, mediation, agreements, contracts, and treaties.

Stage Fourteen: *The Crossing of the Return Threshold.* The trick in returning is to retain the wisdom gained on the quest, to integrate that wisdom into a human life, and then maybe figure out how to share the wisdom with the rest of the world. This stage is a natural continuation of the previous stage. In coaching processes, the focus here is on skills for negotiation and partnerships in a win-win situation. At this stage, experienced, success proven people consider qualifying themselves as consultants, coaches, lecturers, teachers, or authors. The stage is 'Masculine' oriented as it involves values and discipline.

Stage fifteen: *Master of Two Worlds.* This step is usually represented by a transcendental hero like Jesus or Buddha. For a human hero, it may mean achieving a balance between the material and spiritual. The person has become comfortable and competent in both the inner and outer worlds. The sense of mastery leads to freedom from the fear of death, which in turn grants the freedom to live. This is sometimes referred to as living in the moment, neither anticipating the future nor regretting the past. In coaching it is expected to discuss how to enjoy free time, spiritual activities, family pleasure, community or marital interrelationships.

Case study: The Hero J.

reported by: M.M, A graduate of the Jungian Coaching School, Greece, Businesswoman and owner of hotels.

J. was brought up in a poor area of Athens. He attended the local public school. He graduated from college as a social worker. After completing his army duties, he is wondering about his next career move. One day, as he is walking down the street, he comes across an event for volunteers for Médecins sans Frontières. Without any hesitation he signs up and his hero quest begins. This is his "Call for Adventure". He is ready to accept this call.

Within a short period of time, he is offered permanent employment from MSF. His passion for humanitarian work, his intelligence and strong leadership skills help him become director of the local branch. The next stage finds him director of operations for all the programs of MSF. He is the first director in the history of the organization who is not a doctor. He operates in Serbia bombings, Turkey after the earthquakes, in Mozambique, in Zambia, in Georgia and Armenia. These missions are his road of trials. Part of his duties is to decide who will receive medical treatment from the scarce resources available. He has to choose who lives and who is left to die. J. has gone through a long "Road of Trials" and arrived at the top of the "The Meeting with the Goddess". Upon returning from one of these missions, he is so sad and overwhelmed from the atrocities, the human suffering and paranoia of war. Apparently, J. has fallen into the "Woman as Temptress" on the aspect of "power". This stage regresses him inevitably to the "Belly of the Whale"; He stays in his room staring at the ceiling chipping with his finger a small crack on the wall, num from pain. He wants to help more; he wants to be based and operating in his own country. He is stuck.

In 2004, he started his own NGO. At this point he arrives at the "Return" stage in the Hero quest. In the beginning the NGO has only polyclinics treating people without enquiries about the legality of their residence. Having gained the experience of the MSF he now turns the stage of the "Magic Flight" towards "Rescue from Without". Any person in need can visit the clinics and receive treatment free of charge. This approach is typical of the

"Rescue Without" stage on the hero quest. He works incredibly hard for long hours per day to secure private funding and to expand the scope of activities and programs of the NGO. At the same time, he pursues a master's degree in Health Management and Finance. On the Hero quest sequences we find J in the Nirvana Apotheothis (stage 10) which is characterized by voluntary work, spiritual activity or education towards a certificate. The NGO continues to grow and becomes a leader in providing relief for socio-economically vulnerable populations. Furthermore, the NGO advocates strongly for human rights, for LGBT rights, for HIV prevention awareness, for every injustice towards these populations.

By 2017, the NGO has grown exponentially, with more than 100.000 beneficiaries per year, 120 employees and 580 volunteers. He is a PhD prospect. He teaches at the University and part of his research becomes published. He is awarded for his social work and contribution to the vulnerable populations. This is quite an impressive description of stages 12–14 on the hero quest. He is a charismatic and inspirational leader. In his personal life he remains humble, grateful, focused and optimistic. In every room he enters he brings light. He is a "Master of Two Worlds".
The end is sad and unfair for the kind of great hero he is. He died of a galloping form of cancer at the age of 47, leaving a great legacy, his NGO. His life was a continuous hero quest. An example of a hero with a purpose larger than serving his needs.

Chapter 26

The Hero Quest – more theory and practice

"You should carry the monastery in yourself. The desert is within you. The desert calls you and draws you back. Truly, I prepare you for solitude".

Red Book, Liber Primus (pg. 230)

Netzer (2011) claims that the fact that the Hero has turned into a myth proves that the Hero encounters immense powers within the psyche; unconscious powers that support or threaten the person. He copes with them and creates the existence and development of the Conscious Ego. This process is described in the mythos as "combating the monster or dragon" in various ways, symbolizing the chaotic, unknown, and powerful forces in the psyche and the struggle to overcome them. The mythos describes the dynamics in the psyche, the movement between developmental forces and regression, between being swallowed and bursting forth, between destruction and redemption. A catalog of Netzer's collection of steps in the Hero Quest may help the Jungian coach locate the client's "story" (brought in a coaching session) in his Hero Quest's appropriate stage. Taking those steps symbolically will point out at the requisite of the coping skills in moving on with the coachee's quest. Here are Netzer's Hero Quest stages and their applied coaching considerations:

It starts with prophecy about the Hero's birth (*in coaching when a client claims: "this job has always meant for me…"*). *It* continues with magic and the modest birth of the Hero (*in coaching: when a client is "adopted" by a patron*). Double parents: besides noble parents, the hero has humble parents (*in coaching the difference between biological parent to a significant mentor*). The exile from paradise (*client was fired or relocated or moved to another sector*); departure from Mother (*in coaching, any move from comfort zone*), the experience of abandonment, rejection and being orphaned (*disappearance of a protecting boss, end of studies and need to be absorbed in the free market*), facing the threat of extinction (*downsizing, discharge, short of budget*). Great mother protects the hero, rescues him symbolized by big animals (*well-off conditions granted to employees, promotion, shares*). Onset

DOI: 10.4324/9780429351518-26

of hero's magical powers, childhood omnipotence (*proven success, out-standing exit in early age!*). Belief in self and omnipotence, grandiose feelings and a child's magical powers (*inflated Ego phenomena*). Coping with brother's jealousy (*competition between peers in a corporation*). Trickster: resourcefulness, tricks, shrewdness for survival or rebellion (*unethical manipulative and political acts in a corporation*). Departure for a distant destination such as a forest, country, sky, underworld (*relocation*). Fighting against monstrous great mothers (*in coaching the inevitable required response to tolerate a one-sided abusive act imposed by the company or its representatives, or facing one own's Shadow; inferiorities, fears and curruption*). Departure from mother: search for a father figure, identification with father principle and its values (*setting up for or acquiring professional education*). Acquisition of the potential to restrain, control, sublimate drives and emotions according to cultural law (*socialization at work standards, assimilating to a new professional environment*). Acquisition of ethics, morality, and consciousness with either sin or guilt feelings (*any voluntary or inevitable interactions with the law or registrations connected to moral and ethical issues*). Overcoming initiation assignments to prove courage, overcoming suffering, restraint and avoiding temptations in order to strengthen the Ego (*deadlines, recruitments, competitive acts, aggressive business initiatives, open market struggles*). Connectedness, attachment to a significant other, social absorption (*mentoring or nonprofitable organization's activities – NGO*). Overcoming in the fight against a threatening monster or representatives of dreadful father images (*Corona pandemic, business crises, economic depression*). Rebelling against society and father's authority, stealing wisdom, individuation and aloneness (*separating from company, opening one's own business*). Exit for protecting the weak and underprivileged. Serving as shepherd, a preliminary stage towards taking over responsibility and leadership (*NGO voluntary leadership*). Mentors – such as animals, wise coach, God. Receiving advice and gifts which possess a protecting/ fighting potential such as a rod, ring, talisman, amulet, shield, or sword (*coaching, consultation, psychotherapy*). Appearance of an identical twin brother or duplicate, complimentary figures who operate together (*successful partnership, peering, teamwork*). Woman's redemption or attachment to the Feminine side – Anima. (*in coaching; the ability to involve emotions in decision processes*). Actualization of love, matrimony and family (*in coaching the challenge to balance the personal with the professional, the Masculine with Feminine under the Conjunctio archetype*). Finding the treasure that is the reservoir of inner assets. Work, self-actualization and professional career (*challenging oneself with studies, extended education and expansion of knowledge*). Coping against pride – hubris. Searching for meaning and spiritual self-actualization (*balancing the materialistic drive with spiritual routine activity*). Establishing new creative elements: founding a city, social structure or theory (*Hi tech start-ups*). Returning home and granting wisdom to tribes or community (*voluntary, philanthropic involvement*). Returning to the inner savage potential in the psyche *(in coaching, connecting to the instinctive, spontaneous, sensational elements in the coachee's personality)*. Accepting limitations and reconciliation *(in coaching a mature outcome as a result of Shadow work)*. A betrayal, collapse or a heroic sacrifice, or premature death – all of which bestow a tragic or heroic aura (in coaching *overcoming bankruptcy, sudden loss of a significant leader in company, physical disaster*). Religious dimension: acceptance of aging and death and preparation for the final journey (*retirement*)" (pp. 26–38).

Netzer identifies eight types of Heroes: hero with physical superpowers, hero as trickster, hero castrated by mother (Puer Aeternus), hero of many valorous plots, hero in search of his Anima, hero in search of his savage, natural instinctual–sensory side, hero in a religious process, mature, moderate hero in second part of life.

In coaching, once fitting the client's story to the exact hero-stage, the coach can sort out which coaching tools to offer the client. *Example; In a private firm two brothers are in severe conflict and both seek out business coaching. This story fits with 'coping brother's jealousy'.*

Of great importance is the comparison Netzer makes between the hero and the Ego (chapter 15) claiming that basic Ego forces are vital to heroism. (*This long list of Ego-Hero traits can serve the Jungian coach as an **evaluative questionnaire** to help figure out which of the traits the client needs to develop. If the client is a woman, she can develop her Animus repertoire accordingly.*) Restraint, self-discipline, control, tolerance, coping with physical suffering and difficulties, decisiveness, persistency, determination, will power, execution, initiative, courage, responsibility, commitment, patience, absorption, flexibility, rational thinking, differential consciousness. All those traits are attributed to the Masculine Principle database. "The Hero is the Ego", states Netzer,

> characterized by masculine traits, breaking through in order to release himself from the mother's bosom, from a state of passivity, warmth, enveloping, and from the preconscious phase. The hero is the phallus that bursts forth, intrudes, and conquers. Moving forwards towards the future. The fighter, the active initiator, director, planner, activator. The Ego – hero is a competitive achiever, possesses the drive to succeed, with a will, power, ambition, tolerance and passivity. On those assignments she counts the fighting hero, rebellious hero, cultural hero, hero as a Leader, charismatic hero, shaman, the artist as hero, modern heroes, mechanical hero and science fiction hero. (pp. 47–92)

In corresponding with the Belly of the Whale (5th stage on the Hero Quest), Netzer (2011) stresses the inevitable experience every coachee must go through, namely; aloneness and solitude. "By being alone", argues Netzer, "one arrives at the insights that 'I am who I am' and sees the variance be-tween 'oneself and others'. The discovery of one's own individuality is both frightening and exciting". The Jungian coach must accept that eventually both the coachee as much as the coach are lonely.

> We can deceive ourselves or be mistaken or pretend that it is not so, but how important it is to admit, that indeed we are lonely. Turn your aloneness into your preliminary state of existence, love your loneliness and bear the suffering it causes you...so that your aloneness will serve you in the most peculiar moments as a source of support from which you will find the right solutions. (pp. 97–108)

Every transitional stage in life creates an encounter with loneliness anxiety and may turn into a crisis unless there are preliminary inner psychic struc-tures that enable the containment of our aloneness. This is a crucial point. The real challenges are not external forces in the outside reality world. In Jungian Coaching the coachee eventually always finds out that the real destructive power is located in the internal personal psyche.

Another aspect of the Hero Quest, relevant to coaching, is the theme of the mythological monster/dragon who designates the destructive, passionate aspect of the hero's unconscious.

> It symbolizes the bestial instinctual drive of the human being. Killing or destroying the monster does not mean killing the unconscious' drives and passions, but rather overcoming their additional destructive power. Connecting to monsters means being in touch with every drive or feeling which threatens to overcome the human being's "powerful weaknesses". The Ego is built up by learning to restrain oneself and channel the drives and emotions in an efficient manner. Animals present the passionate impulsive side of the human psyche. Unlike the monster that is to be either killed or stopped, the friendly animal may have positive aspects symbolizing instincts that lead the psyche. One needs to learn to train them (the animals = the coachee's instincts), befriend with them and harness them to the psyche's chariot. (pp. 109–112)

What is the psychological role of the coach in this coaching quest?

It is the coach's role to mediate the "internal coach", the Self archetype, and its Father principle database to the client. Netzer (2011, p. 112) suggests that "Teachers along the road represent those aspects of the psyche that until the moment we encountered with them were absent in our consciousness. We need to listen to them". The coach must usher the coachee to encounter his own inner coach, meaning; The Self (chapter 15). "The Self sends its wisdom through the bestial (instinctual), the shadowy, spiritual, feminine or mascu-line, wise, the childish or magical power. The 'Self' corresponds with the 'The Father' principle" (p. 113). In coaching, the Masculine-Father principle encounters the coach-coachee with issues connected to the role of the boss, system considerations and demands, collaboration with a mentor and supervisor. (*I should stress again that when speaking about the Father Principle we refer to the psychological principles and not the gender, as a woman can hold a father psychological role as well*). Netzer (2011): "The law puts limits to drives and emotions; It defines order and organization as well as forms and structures the personal and the social. The Father Principle decides upon relationships, upon the level of restraint versus spontaneity, flexibility and tolerance versus rigidity, sanctions and punishments. The Father Principle also creates hierarchy and democracy in the family, forms sociality and organizations. It designs the style of authority, extent of freedom for personal thinking, speech and behavior, approaches intuition, creativity, initiatives and innovations, imprints sacred codes, values for religion and faith, mythos and rituals, relationships between state and individual, relationship between the individual and the collective. Ideals such as truth, justice, decency, honesty, responsibility, investment, tolerance, altruism, good, loyalty and respect. Paternal values are dictated by the Father Principle, they count also in hygiene, body, sexuality, materialism, property, land, work, nature, psyche, soul, spirit, superstitions, time, divinity and death. This Masculine Principle targeted towards children, the elderly, the weak, the invalid, the sick, the stranger, towards women, women's values, relationship between men and women, education and initiations, all that is in the domain of ideology, ethics, religion, politics, administration, sociology and education."

One crucial factor has to do with the Hero and his Anima. (The Heroine and her Femininity is demonstrated nicely through Gwendoline Tracey Philippa Christie the English actress and model. She is best known for portraying Brienne of Tarth in the HBO fantasy-drama series *Game of Throne*). One of the Hero quest outcomes is the release of the repressed Femininity and shifting from the Great Mother's domain (unconscious) into the Feminine territory (being able to be in intimate relationships). This means in practical coaching to help the coachee discover his or her Femininity. We speak here mostly about emotional involvement, an ability to tolerate longitudinal processes and capability for relatedness. Why "shift it from the Great Mother's domain?" Netzer (2011) answers:

Because as long as the Femininity is denied or repressed, metaphorically it is considered held in the dark unconscious. Successful women are challenged not to be possessed by their Animus and balance their personality with their Femininity. Wherelse, a well developed Anima calms men, provides tenderness, sensitivity, intuition, expression of feelings, warmth, patience, contact with the senses, with nature, connectedness to the unconscious, to the magical and mysterious as well as the supernatural and spiritual. A positive integrated Anima, which mediates man's consciousness to his inner world, is indeed the function which connects him to his actual feminine female partner in his life. Through a well developed positive Anima, man can create mutual relationships and perceive the woman not as a trapping figure or a suffering creature but rather as a partner and individual.

Clear illustration for Hero-Anima relatedness can be seen in *Gladiator*, a 2000 epic historical drama film directed by Ridley Scott, starring Russell Crowe. The physical Hero there surrenders to his wife's psyche, which functions as his Anima.

Chapter 27

Twenty-four leadership archetypes in teamwork

"Our Gods want to be overcome, since they require renewal. If men kill their princess, they do so because they cannot kill their Gods, and because they do not know that they should kill their Gods in themselves".

Red Book, Liber Primus (pg. 242)

This chapter deals with the theory and practice of coaching with teams, board, groups, and target-oriented groups. The 24 leadership archetypes cover the whole spectrum of corporate issues. We can practice executives coaching as well as with team coaching. The tool offers the coachee an opportunity to expand his or her potential, evolving undeveloped or dormant personality traits. The idea is to arrive at the maximum extended spectrum of the client or the team's available behavior. Following the "Economic Model" (chapter 5) we can grasp the whole organization under the 24 leadership archetype paradigm. Once again Jungian Coaching targets its coaching skills to assist the coachee or the team in dealing with their inferiority, heading toward the expansion of the coachee's or the team's leadership traits.

Corlett and Pearson (2003) present in their book *Mapping the Organizational Dynamics and Change* a comprehensive picture on the archetypal psychic anatomy and structure of the organization. They propose four domains designating four different managerial responsibilities in the organization.

The upper part of the circle relates to human resources in the organization: People (H.R – for human resource operations, for which Jungian Coaching Method attributed the "water", symbolizing "emotions") and Learning (R&D – for research and development, symbolized by "air", for inspiration, creativity and inventiveness). The lower part of the circle presents Stabilizing (CEO – regulations and management, symbolized by "earth", for infrastructure) and Results (CFO – relates to revenue and profits, marketing, branding and advertisement, symbolized by "fire" for high energetic investment). On the upper part (dealing with people, research,

DOI: 10.4324/9780429351518-27

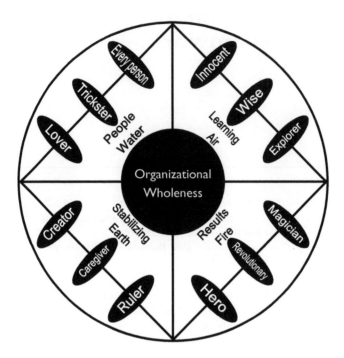

Figure 27.1 The Organizational Structure, Based on Corlett and Pearson (2003).

and learning) Corlett and Pearson (2003) suggested 3 + 3 archetypes, to present the required and expected traits for executives who operate on those domains. This gallery of required archetypal traits predicts what qualities an executive should possess, in order to interact effectively with people and to manage development and research competencies. This gallery not only includes "common archetypes" such as the Hero, Trickster, Anima, Animus and Persona but also offers additional characters.

As with the Hero Jungian Coaching Cards, here as well we offer the coachee to practice the 24 Leadership cards by activating them through a dialogue (the archetype presented in the card holds a deep, authentic and courgous conversation with the coachee). We encourage the client to speak to the archetype, relate to its traits and check which of the archetypal characteristics are worth adopting and assimilating. In the dialogue, during the coaching session, the moment the coachee "becomes" the selected archetype, identifies with him/her traits and puts forwards its argumentations, a dramatic change on the awareness level and in the coachee's behavior is manisested.

We see that the "Lover", "Trickster", "Wise", and "Explorer" archetypes alongside "Every-Person" (conformist who functions "by the book") traits seem essential in human interactions. Articulating to archetypes, we should consider not only those "positive" derivative traits of the archetypes (offered by Corlett, J. and Pearson) but the Shadow archetypal aspect as well; the "negative" opposing traits that correspond to those offered by Corlet and Pearson. This means that we should sometimes embrace in coaching the "negative-attributed" behaviors or acts of the archetype's shadow as vital, in order to operate effectively in an overall personal and professional life. Example:

PEOPLE – HUMAN RESOURCE – WATER

The Lover Archetype. On its "positive side" the card says:

LOVER ARCHETYPE – VALUES

- *I am emotionally intelligence*
- *I have personal attractiveness*
- *I possess a sense of community*
- *I make consensual decisions*

I AM GOOD AT

- *Fostering a sense of real caring among employees*
- *Treating each employee as special*
- *Building positive relationship with customers*
- *Getting everyone's input on decisions*

On the 'negative' aspect, the Shadow of the Lover archetype, the coachee copes with the following card:

MY SHADOW IS:

- *I do not separate the personal from the professional*
- *I do not deal with conflict*
- *I will never take unpopular stand*
- *It's hard to me to respect other people*

Often, a "Lover personality" will find that owning the Shadow traits are quite a challenging growth.
   For Trickster Archetype picture and text look up chapter 23.
   In counterpart to the Lover archetype stands the Trickster, which enables the coachee to mediate between the personal approach (employee-oriented) and the systemic organizational interests. Some coachees are trickster-oriented by nature, and others may find that adopting such an approach is unethical or evil. The Trickster archetype card claims:

TRICKSTER ARCHETYPE - VALUES

- *I find ways to make work fun*
- *I am full of playful inventiveness*
- *I can easily manipulate*
- *seeing clever ways around obstacles*

I AM GOOD AT:

- *Brainstorming*
- *Lightening people up*
- *Accelerating processes*
- *Allowing a flexible work schedule*

MY SHADOW IS:

- *It is hard for me to plan ahead*
- *I hate to get paperwork done*
- *I will act unethically if needed*
- *I can not resist making a joke at someone's expense*

The third archetype in the People's domain is Everyperson. Connecting to the "ordinary" is an essential trait that stands along with the two charged and dynamic archetypes (Lover & trickster) to deliberately assure ethical professional behavior. The Every Person card says:

EVERY PERSON ARCHETYPE – VALUES:

- *I have respect towards every person*
- *I am solid at work and unpretentious*
- *I am bending together to survive tough times*
- *I am willing to work for a monthly salary*

I AM GOOD AT:

- *Rewarding employees who try*
- *Treating everybody equally*
- *Implementing fair employment policies*
- *Being empathic with employees*

MY SHADOW IS:

- *I do not search for advancement opportunities*
- *I do not seek support pleasures*

- *I do not demand myself to work hard and effectively*

When coaching executives who work in the research and development do-main, we first encounter with the Wise archetype. The Wise archetype on its "positive" and "negative" sides will challenge the coachee to hold a dialogue with the following:

WISE ARCHETYPE - VALUES

- *I have broad knowledge*
- *I possess expert knowledge in many areas*
- *I strive for quality results*
- *I can create and lead learning*

I AM GOOD AT

- *Fostering continuous learning*
- *Putting evaluation processes in place*
- *Implementing research and development*
- *Analyzing complex issues*

MY SHADOW IS:

- *I hate to deal with people who do not seem wise*
- *I must act only after all facts are in and analyzed*
- *I see through someone who sounds intelligent but is off track*
- *I anticipate people's feeling responses*

Besides having a broad know-how and experience, it is expected from an executive in the R&D domain to be creative and connected with the Explorer archetype.

THE EXPLORER ARCHETYPE – VALUES

- **I am independent**
- **I am self starter**
- **I am a pioneer**
- **I believe in authenticity**

I AM GOOD AT:

- *Supporting employees autonomy*
- *Discouraging conformist thinking*
- *Minimizing bureaucracy*

- *Seeking out new ideas and perspective*

MY SHADOW IS:

- *I can not lead coordinative activities*
- *I don't like to be a team player*
- *I hate to keep everyone informed*
- *I do not pay enough attention to staff to supervise them adequately*

To assure that the products, provisions, and inventions are made according to regulated standards under legal authorized procedures, those executives must be connected to the Innocent archetype.

THE INNOCENT ARCHETYPE – VALUES

- *I am loyal*
- *I follow the rules*
- *I am open and honest*

I AM GOOD AT:

- *Providing clear guidance to employees*
- *Offering employees long-term security*
- *Training employees to do things right*
- *Taking care after employees*

MY SHADOW IS:

- *I do not encourage innovation*
- *It's difficult for me to deal with problematic employees*
- *I do not face problems until they escalate*
- *I do not deal with complex problems*

Looking at the lower gallery, we see that in order to function in the organizational management we must set up standards, ethics, norms, and regulations. The required archetypal traits are "Ruler", "Caregiver", and "Creator" (both "positive" and "negative") and for the "money making" domain, one needs to acquire the archetypal traits of "Hero", "Revolutionary", and "Magician" (both "positive" and "negative").

We registered a reservoir of *24 leadership profile traits* (12 offered by Corlett, J. and Pearson, C., and 12 are corresponding and compensating Shadow traits). With this magic archetypal repertoire, the Jungian coach can tutor a coachee to connect, develop and improve his or her managerial or behavior skills. Later in this chapter we shall demonstrate how to work with the 24 archetypes in groups.

When a coachee refers and describes difficulties in management or in life challenges in within the context of an organization (corporations, family, team) the Jungian coach helps the coachee to:

1. Locate himself or herself on the domain he or she operates from.
2. Sort out both the "positive" and "negative" leadership cards in that domain.
3. Find out which out of the six cards the coachee naturally possesses, and which are his or her "inferior functional archetypes", those which are underdeveloped and which will be coached on.
4. Check which card he or she will need in order to practice in the "here and now", by "becoming", activating, developing and finally owning that archetypal trait he or she lacks.

In small business or in the case of self-employment, it is expected to embrace all 12 archetypal traits, including their negative repertoires. Obviously, this is quite challenging, explaining why it is difficult to run a business by oneself.

Here are two examples for the coaching with the leadership cards.

On an individual level: *A competent CEO of a five-star hotel in a peripheral city has moved to the capital with an intention to change her career. She is looking for business opportunities apart from hotel and tourism of which she claimed to have had enough of. In her recent job she was connected and maneuvered successfully through the positive archetypes of the Creator, Caregiver, Ruler, Hero, Revolutionary, and the Magician archetypes (managing and profiting mostly). Apparently she did very well connecting naturally to these managerial talents. Let us look at those traits:*

THE CREATOR ARCHETYPE – VALUES:

*   *I am very creative*
*   *I produce creative products*
*   *I strive for a unique outlook*
*   *I have very good (aesthetic) taste*

I AM GOOD AT:

*   *Fostering creating teams*
*   *Encouraging creative products*
*   *Allowing employees the freedom to be imaginative*
*   *Taking an imaginative approach to life and work*

MY SHADOW IS:

- *I can not focus on non-creative activities*
- *I can not avoid innovation to what can be produced and marketed*
- *It is impossible for me to say no to promising ideas*
- *It's hard for me to refrain from prima-donna behaviors*

THE CAREGIVER ARCHETYPE – VALUES

- *I always show care for others*
- *I sacrifice for the greatest good*
- *I am available for others*
- *I will help those most in need*

I AM GOOD AT:

- *Caring for others*
- *Customer service jobs*
- *inspiring employees to be caring for one another*
- *Providing a warm, nurturing environment*

MY SHADOW IS:

- *I can not say no to anyone in need*
- *I do not assess the cost to the staff before making commitment*
- *I find it difficult to require from others to be as self-reliant as possible*
- *I do not acknowledge my own limits*

THE RULER ARCHETYPE – VALUES

- *I am providing the standards others will follow*
- *I have political leadership experience*
- *I radiate prestige and power*
- *I know how to get things done*

I AM GOOD AT:

- *Fostering clear lines of authority*
- *Being a strong leader*
- *Deciding other people destiny*
- *Putting system in place to ensure timely and quality results*

MY SHADOW IS:

- *I create overly complex bureaucratic processes*
- *I can not deal fairly with people who challenge my authority*
- *I hate acknowledge my mistakes*
- *I hate office politics because I want the work to be done*

THE HERO ARCHETYPE – VALUES

- *I create a team spirit feeling*
- *I consistently come through challenges*
- *I do achieve goals*
- *I do posses the toughness to get the job done*

I AM GOOD AT:

- *Getting things done*
- *Creating clear goals and outcomes*
- *Motivating people to work hard*
- *Coaching the team on how to succeed*

MY SHADOW IS:

- *I can not possibly walk away from challenge*
- *I will not slow down and re-evaluate*
- *I will hardly respect the perspective of someone who disagrees with me*
- *I will not sympathize with someone who seems like a loser*

THE REVOLUTIONARY ARCHETYPE – VALUES

- *I have radical ideas and practice*
- *I favor radical innovative change*
- *I am a critical spirit*
- *I continually question how things are done*

I AM GOOD AT:

- *Thinking differently*
- *Taking risks*
- *Considering people's wilder ideas*
- *Executing radical innovation*

MY SHADOW IS:

- *I do not stick to established practices*
- *I will not keep my mouth shut*
- *I do not get along with conventional people*
- *I do not learn from the past mistakes*

MAGICIAN ARCHETYPE – VALUES

- *I am self aware*
- *I will always stand for Win\win solution*
- *I arrive to seemingly miraculous outcomes*
- *I am a catalyst for change*

I AM GOOD AT:

- *Reframing problems as opportunities*
- *Being charismatic*
- *Vision clarification*
- *Allowing flexibility in how groups accomplish goal*

MY SHADOW IS:

- *I believe that a miracle may pull things out at the last moment*
- *I have no limit aspirations*
- *It is hard for me to distinguish a complex idea from a solid one*
- *I am not interested in supervision*

In the transition phase of her professional life she is expected to shift into the Learning and Research domains where different alternative archetypal traits are required. She is expected to expand her personality and be in touch with the "Lover", "Trickster", "Wise"; and "Explorer"; alongside "Every-person" (conformist by the book) traits. Some she will connect easily with and others she might need coaching to adopt to, as they do not connect to power but rather to modesty, obedience, and openness. In the coaching process, if only one single archetypal trait is added successfully to a client's availability, it makes huge changes in his or her potential.

Let us observe another example on the team level: *In a board of directors meeting the CEO is expressing his disappointment that the quarterly report shows a loss trend. The H.R representative expresses her concern as just recently they dismissed a few employees, the CFO is pressing on the*

R&D Manager to commit for the expected deadline of launching the new product, hoping it will change the financial picture.

For this team to function effectively, these are the required archetypal traits expected to be manifested in the meeting: The HR representative must connect to her "Trickster" archetypal traits (otherwise it is very likely she will suffer ricochets from the CEO). The R&D Manager must connect to his "Wise" and "Explorer" in order to affiliate with the CFO and create an intensive unified team to accelerate the production of the expected product. The CEO, if he wishes to overcome the crises, would better not approach with the antagonistic "Ruler" archetypal behavior but rather connect to the "Creator".

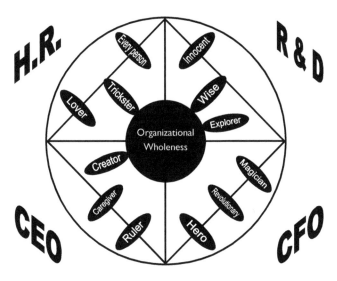

Figure 27.2 The ideal archetypal picture to cope in this stressful meeting, based on Corlett and Pearson (2003).

This would have happened if the company had used the consultation of a Jungian Coach who had practiced awareness to pitfalls with the Team. However, in reality, the following picture might occur: The CEO falls unfortunately into his Shadow (as his Ego is weak and tense in this situation). He will inevitably connect to the negative side of the "Ruler". The CFO protects himself and alliances with the CEO by connecting to the negative sides of the "Revolutionary" and "Hero". The HR representative is overwhelmed and spontaneously represents the employees through the "Lover" and "Every Person" archetypes, and this overall energy, very likely, will paralyze the R&D Manager who under such conditions cannot connect to the positive "Explorer" and the "Wise" archetypes and regresses to the negative side of the "Innocent" archetype.

Figure 27.3 The unfortunate archetypal picture displayed in this stressful meeting, based on Corlett and Pearson (2003).

Let's imagine the CEO, following that explosive meeting, referred to Jungian Coaching. In the technique of activating the archetype (chapter 2) he would have practiced the state of: "I am a 'Care - Giver'. In a time of stress, I can enable my team to work hard as I support them, containing my concerns and supporting them in obscure conditions...". A dialogue between the positive "Caregiver Archetype" and the CEO will establish a mature aspect in the manager's personality that can support him (self-supporting internal system) in such stressful situations at work.

Here is a structured method to apply Jungian Coaching with a team in a corporation. This board demonstrates the archetypes (active or passive, conscious or unconscious) presented in any team, board, or staff meeting.

The Leadership Observation Form enables the coach to evaluate the active dominant archetypes displayed by the participants in a board or a team meeting. By identifying the *spontaneous current overt archetypes* that activate the participants in a meeting, the Jungian coach can identify the "saboteurs" archetypes that create communicative obstacles. Obviously the coach is expected to be acquainted with the 12 leadership archetypes and their shadows. If the team agrees upon the meeting's agenda then it is possible for the

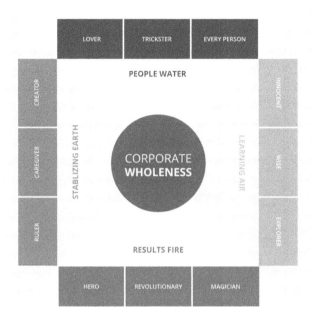

Figure 27.4 Presented Archetypes in Teamwork.

coach to estimate the expected dominant archetypes required from each participant according to his or her role.

On the upper left is the CEO functioning domain, characterized by the positive and negative options of the Ruler, Caregiver, and Creator archetypes. The attached filled up Observation Form displays an example for a meeting. In this particular session we can see that the Jungian coach labeled the CEO as *dominant on the positive Ruler archetype but inferior on the Caregiver and Creator positive archetypes.* This means that the CEO has an underdeveloped Anima and we can predict that his interpersonal relationships are limited yet his management is fair. In the executive coaching the Jungian coach will discuss with the CEO the option to activate and experience his Feminine underdeveloped archetypes of the Caregiver and the Creator.

If we move on to the lawyer left, we observe the CFO, with the Hero, Revolutionary, and Magician positive and negative archetypal traits. In this session the CFO is apparently observed as *very active with ideas, thinking out of the box and risk taking, as he is dominant on the Revolutionary and Magician archetypal levels. However the Jungian coach found out that his Hero leadership is negatively inferior, meaning on the one hand the CFO brings up too many ideas yet on the other hand he lacks leadership style.* In

CEO Stabilization		R&D Development and Research		Other	
Ruler +	→ Dominant	Explorer +	→ Inferior		→
Ruler -	→	Explorer -	→		→
Caregiver +	→ Inferior	Wise +	→ Dominant		→
Caregiver -	→	Wise -	→		→
Creator +	→ Inferior	Innocent +	→ Dominant		→
Creator -	→	Innocent -	→		→
Hero +	→ Inferior	Everyperson +	→ Dominant		
Hero -	→ Inferior	Everyperson -	→		
Revolutionary +	→ Dominant	Trickster +	→ Inferior		
Revolutionary -	→	Trickster -	→		
Magician +	→ Dominant	Lover +	→ Dominant		
Magician -	→	Lover -	→		
CFO Results		H.R. People			

Figure 27.5 Presented Observation Form.

coaching he will be advised to explore the Hero Quest cards on the Road of Trial stage (chapter 25).

On the upper right side of the Observation Form we see the R&D profile with the Explorer, Wise, and Innocent positive and negative archetypes. In this session the Jungian coach's impression is that the R&D is *not connected to the Explorer archetype (inferior), she lacks basic knowledge (Dominant negative side of the Wise) and is too conformist (Dominant Positive Innocent archetype).* This poor performance is not typical of an executive who is in charge of innovation, research, and development. It might be attributed to her being new on this job. In coaching it would be advisable to check her response to the profile obtained and her actual needs.

The profile of the HR displays on the lawyer right side of the Observation Form an HR who *operates very much by the book (Dominant Every Person archetype), very naive (Positive Trickster archetype is Inferior) while she is very lovable (Dominant Lover archetype).*

Here is the practical coaching conclusion the Jungian coach may arrive at intervening through executive coaching with each of the four members of the team: Following the staff meeting, the Jungian coach can meet for an individual Jungian executive coaching with each of the participants. In this individual coaching the coach shows the executive his "archetypal profile" and explains to the coachee how those archetypes served him or sabotaged his conduct. The Observation Form helps both the coach and coachee to figure out which archetypes should have been used in serving a better directorial job, meaning which archetype was found inferior (underdeveloped). By practicing and activating the inferior archetypes (chapter 2) the executive expands his or her behavioral profile with which he or she will return to the next meeting with a new approach. Such innovative approach changes dramatically the communication, goodwill, and collaboration among the team.

Chapter 28

The dream as an internal coach

"Dreams are the guiding words of the soul".

Red Book, Liber Primus (pg. 233)

At times, right at the first meeting, or other times while in the course of the coaching process, the coachee may come up with a dream that is somehow connected to the dilemma for which he or she referred to coaching. In Jungian Coaching we should grasp the content of the dream as a validated content that derived from the unconscious through the transcendent function and try to: (1) understand its symbolic meaning (the images and acts in the dream) and how they possibly connect to the client's topic (chapter 3), (2) compare the dream's content to the choachee's Persona-Ego point of view (chapters 15, 17), and (3), most important, ask the coachee: "What do you think this dream wishes to tell you concerning the dilemma you face these days"?

Stein (1998) writes that "dreams are made out of these unconscious images and complexes" (41), and Samuels (1985) tells us that in relating to dreams, "Jung's disagreement with Freud was over the question of manifest and latent dream content, *Jung looked at dreams content as psychic facts*" (p. 230). The application of Samuel's statement to coaching applies in that we have to take the coachee's dream seriously and relate it as an unconscious material to elaborate on. The myth is the tribe's dream, while the dream is the individual's myth, said Jung. The dream in Jungian Coaching can be taken as a gift because it is a spontaneous unconscious content, and practically can convey a message, give direction and original advice to the coachee. Freud considered the unconscious as a "psychic warehouse", containing repressed childhood traumatic events, charging in return the price of hysteria or neurosis for keeping it "down" there protected by mechanisms of defense. Jung agreed partially with this role of the unconscious, but further believed the unconscious, in addition, is connected to the collective unconscious, and is an autonomous creative reservoir of drives, ideas,

DOI: 10.4324/9780429351518-28

symbols, and images that strives to actualize itself through dreams, arts, and acts. Von Franz and Boa (1988), in their outstanding book, *The Way of the Dream* , say:

> Each one of the thousands of dreams we have during our lifetime is unique. Some seem straightforward while others are complex, but all dreams are spontaneous and unpredictable. It is surprising to observe therefore that many dreams do in fact have an identifiable structure, a framework in which the dream is organized. When we trace the outline of that structure, the random flow of images and events begins to fall into place. (p. 40)

In Jungian terms, one devotes to a "dream work", meaning, trying to decipher the hidden message that the dream holds for the coachee. It is advisable to encourage the client to draw the dream of fragments of the dream. This correlates to A. Robbins (1989) approach in his "Aesthetic distancing" (chapter 4).

There are three functions of the dream. The first function is the *Compensatory Function* (chapter 6). The psyche has a role in balancing itself by providing the dreamer what he or she misses in his or her actual life or vice versa, taking away from him or her what he or she prospers with. Such dreams may help the coach and coachee monitor the coachee's desires and ethics.

The second function of the dream is the *Educating Function*. This function is of great help for the coaching quest. The psyche, through the unconscious SELF, knows what is good for the client; it is always teaching the coachee what should or shouldn't be done. We should keep in mind that the productions of the unconscious are not necessarily adhered to reality and may turn out to be quite a blizzard or irrational experience for the coachee. *Example: A widow in her fifties who suffered from mild depression (which she attributed to the loss of her husband, ten years prior) came to coaching with the initiative to start a second career. In a dream she saw a river; on both sides were forests and wild animals. The forest symbolizes the unconscious (as it is dark, deep, and with a possibility of getting lost there), and the animals represent the instincts with its potential danger - located on both sides of her life quest. In the river, she saw Pocahontas in a boat, "rowing against the stream," she claimed. I was astonished that, at her age, she identified with that instinctual nature figure, who leads her little boat, with one tough paddle, against the stream, against conformity. (She claimed her granddaughter plays with such a miniature). When asked to dialogue with that heroine, the woman consulted with Pocahontas about a new relationship she has started with a man much younger than herself. Again, I was surprised she unconsciously preferred to discuss that issue with Pocahontas and not with me. Pocahontas served as an internal guide. We found out that the woman's psyche (projected onto Pocahontas) urges her to go on with that relationship and move out of her old apartment that she had shared with her late husband. The dream presents to us two young figures, one from unconscious (Pocahontas) and the other from conscious level (young lover). Both intend to usher the client into an innovative path. Now it was just expected to explain to the coachee the symbolic meaning of such a young Animus and the Feminine archetype chosen by her creative unconscious. This insight directed us immediately into innovative ideas about her career. What a deep educating message from such a seemingly simple cartoon movie figure.*

The third function of the dream is rare but exists and it can be overwhelming. This is the *Predicting Dream*. Such dreams are almost impossible to comprehend, and usually they point toward a strong intuition to unexpected events or situations and the far future.

Chapter 29

Jung's psychological types and the MBTI: The dawn of Jungian Coaching

"The thinker's passions are bad; therefore, he has no pleasure. The thoughts of one who feels are bad, therefore he has no thoughts. He who prefers to think than to feel, leaves his feeling to rot in darkness...he who prefers to feel than to think leaves his thinking in darkness, where it spins its nets in gloomy places".

Red Book, Liber Primus (pg. 248)

As a certified MBTI practitioner, I may state that Jungian Coaching starts where the MBTI ends. In corporate life it is quite accustomed to have executives assessed with the "four magic letters" that label them whether they are extroverts or introverts, percievers or judges plus what are their dominant or inferior mental functions. However, assuming one wishes to develop him or herself, what can an executive do with that tag and how does he or she challenge his or her inferiority? At this point, the Jungian Coaching offers the assessed coachee, a variety of coaching options. Once we receive the MBTI results, the Jungian Coach can plan with the coachee a sequence of meetings in order to compensate for his or her inferiorities. For those assessed as F (Feeling) or N (Intuitive) dominant we shall recommend to practice the Masculine Principle tools and for those assessed T (Thinking) or S (Sensational) we would offer the Feminine principle tools.

Originally, in the Editorial Note of Jung's "Psychological Type" (1976), Jung shares: "This work sprang originally from my need to define the ways in which my outlook differed from Freud's and Adler's. In attempting to answer this question, I came across the problem of the types; for it is one psychological type which from the outset determines and limits a person's judgment ... my book is an effort to deal with the relationship of the individual to the world, to people and things" (p. v). This means that Jung himself was interested in comprehending what differs people and how we could explain the variety between individuals. Jung's "Psychological Type" contributes to Jungian Coaching in the sense that it explains why people differ in their behavior styles, in their way of thinking, their mode of

DOI: 10.4324/9780429351518-29

decision making and experiencing Life. Think about a team in a corporation or a startup, in an army unit, a family, a dyad, community – With this theory Jung contributes to the understanding of how people deviate from one another and how one can mediate between people after they acknowledged their Shadow, namely, comprehending that we function from our dominant personality's qualities, and we project (as a result of inferior functions) suspicion, restlessness, and antagonism toward people who are not 'our psychological type'.

Myers and Briggs developed the Myers-Briggs Type Indicator Instrument, which is a Preference Personality Test based on C.G. Jung's Psychological Types Theory. In the MBTI manual (2009) we learn that "in the first (1962) manual, Isabel Myers acknowledged her mother, Katharine C. Briggs, co-author of the MBTI instrument" (p. xix). The Myers-Briggs Preference Test presents to the subject a list of "statement -sentences" for which one is required to either agree or disagree. Apparently, they developed a computer system that finally offers the subject a report with *four letters formula,* which characterizes the person's personality. This equation further signifies which are: First, the *dominant* traits of the person ("function or process that is assumed to be the first developed, most conscious and differentiated and governing force domination one's life"). Second, which are his *auxiliary* traits ("the function or process that is second in importance, and provides balance between two categories: perception and judgement vs. extroversion and introversion"). Third, which is the *tertiary* trait ("the function opposite to the auxiliary function, the one which is less accessible to conscious"). Fourth, the *inferior function.* The inferior function is the most popular trait acting in the Jungian Coaching ("the function opposite to the dominant, called the fourth function, least preferred, *the most unconscious, serving as a potential source of difficulties as well as growth*).

Following Jung, the Myers-Briggs presents to us "two umbrellas": Extrovert/Introvert (*Where* do you prefer to focus your attention) originally presented by Juing, and Judger/Perceiver (*How* do you prefer to live your everyday life), which is their later addition to the paradigm. In between those two "where" and "how" experiences, we are exposed to two axes: the Cognitive Axis (Thinking-Feeling) and the Experiential Axis (Sensing-Intuition) for how people acquire information. Thinking type (denotes a person who makes decisions based on logical, practical based on precedent data), Feeler (makes decisions based on what he feels and what others feel), Sensor (prefers specific answers to specific questions), and Intuitive (thinks about several things at once).

In my studies to become a certified MBTI practitioner I was assessed as "IFNP" personality. This means that I am an Introvert (I), Feeler (F), Intuitive (N) and Perceptive (P). Extroversion, Thinking, Sensing and Judging (ETSJ) – which refer to analyzing, judging by details, calculating and conceptualizing - are traits dwelling in my shadow. They are not in my comfort zone. They are psychic materials located down there in my un-conscious cellar waiting for life challenges or Jungian Coaching tools to activate the archetypes which present those traits: "Father", the Masculine archetype, the Ruler, the Explorer, the Analyzer, the Judge. My Anima (feeling-intuitive) is obviously very developed, I am connected easily to mySelf (as I am an introvert) and I love being by myself. I learn fast (per-ceiver), however, I neglect details (for this I shall need a punctual personal assistant). Jungian Coaching is the laboratory that helps coachees expand their personality toward the auxiliary, tertiary, and inferior functions. The optimistic aspect of Jung's Psychological Types (as are most of his theore-tical paradigms) is that those latent potentials are easy to reach, accessible to develop, and design beautiful horizons for a Hero Quest.

One of the ways to help our clients to expand their personality toward their inferior function is by encountering them with the archetypes that represent their compensatory archetypes, meaning that archetype that stands for the inferior function of the client. By assigning the proper "an-tagonistic archetype" that represents the client's inferiority and by using the activation technique (chapter 2) in the here and now, the coachee can dis-cover the benefits in "owning" his or her opposite trait.

Table 29.1 Shows the Possible Inferior Functions and Their Corresponding Compensatory Archetypes

Inferior function Trait (MBTI)	Compensatory & Empowering Archetype (From 24 leadership) to practice in J.C	Rationale
Extrovert inferiority (meaning the person is **Introvert Dominant**)	Lover (People)	Emotionally intelligent, sense of community, treating each employee as special
Introvert inferiority (meaning the person is **extrovert Dominant**)	Caregiver (Stabilizing)	Show care for others, customer service jobs, inspiring employees to be caring to one another, provide warm, nurturing environment.
Judgmental inferiority (person is **Perceptive Dominant**)	Wise (Learning)	I have broad knowledge, expert knowledge in many areas, quality results, evaluation processes in place, implementing research, and analyzing complex issues.

(Continued)

Table 29.1 (Continued)

Inferior function Trait (MBTI)	Compensatory & Empowering Archetype (From 24 leadership) to practice in J.C	Rationale
Perceptive inferiority (person is **Judgmental Dominant**)	Explorer (Learning) Creator (Stabilizing)	Explorer = Minimizing bureaucracy, discouraging conformist thinking, support autonomy. Creator = very creative, allow freedom to be imaginative, imaginative approach to life and work.
Thinking inferiority (**Feeling Dominant**)	Innocent (Learning)	Loyal, follow rules, clear guidelines, do things right
Feeling inferiority (**Thinking Dominant**)	Caregiver (Stabilizing) and Lover (People)	Caregiver = care for others, sacrifice for greater good, available for others, help those in most need. Lover = emotionally intelligent, make consensual decisions, sense of real caring, treat people as real special.
Intuitive inferiority (**Sensational Dominant**)	Trickster (People)	Playful inventiveness, clever ways around obstacles, brainstorming, flexible.
Sensational inferiority (**Intuitive Dominant**)	Everyperson (People) Innocent (Learning)	Everyperson = solid and unpretentious, treating everybody equally. Innocent = loyal, follow rules, clear guidance, do things right.

Chapter 30

Psychopomp – a coach for the coach

"An old man stood before me. He looked like one of the old prophets".
Red Book, Liber Primus (pg. 245)

At the very end of this book I would like to present the "Psychopomp" archetype. The Greek mythology (Fry, 2018) tells us that:

> The god Hades found to his great delight that the shades of more and more humans began to arrive at his subterranean kingdom. Hermes was assigned a new role – the Arch Psychopomp, or "chief conductor of souls" – a duty he discharged with his customary sprightliness and puckish humor. Though the human population grew, only the most important dead were granted the honor of a personal escort by Hermes, the rest were taken by Thanatos, the grim forbidding figure of Death. (p. 143)

From a Jungian Coaching point of view, some vital personality changes can occur only if we allow ourselves to "cross to the other shore of the river of our personality's boundaries". For that a Psychopomp is required. Crossing to the other side of the river means helping the coachee to expand his or her personality; develop new traits or expected behaviors. We have learned in Alchemy that the Negrado–Mortificatio (chapter 16) technique forces the coachee at times to accept spiritual or partial psychological "death" in order to let go of the trash and stick to the desired. When I ask my clients who their Psychopomp is, each one chooses a different leader, according to their needs. One chooses the Hero archetype, another the Shadow, the third chooses the Anima archetype, and so on. Usually the choice of the Psychopomp archetype serves the coachee as a "compensatory function" assuring he or she maintains contract with his or her inferiority. When inquired to make a contract with their Psychopomp, and investigate its practical conclusions, we get an outlining of their hero quest. Through this revival and the encounter with the Psychopomp the coachees are encouraged to go on processing an individual inner growth.

DOI: 10.4324/9780429351518-30

Figure 30.1 Psychopomp.

To abridge this book, here is a 'Psychopomp Compass' to lead you into your quest to become a Jungian coach: When the coachee expects to deal with his inferiority and weakness, offer her or him a Shadow work.

If the coach wishes to help the coachees (managers, leaders, and corporate employees who expect support and direction) to improve their talents; they should try the 24 leadership archetypes.

When the coach wishes to help the coachees expand his or her approach, behavior, or attitude, it is advisable to consider with them to practice the Anima and Animus, Masculine and Feminine archetypal repertoires.

When change is required, do not hesitate to consider with your client one of the seven Alchemy techniques for transformation.

If the coachee brings up issues that relate to his life or professional career (with an emphasis on process; meaning there is a factor of before and after experience) it would be efficient for the client to experience the Hero Quest stages.

Whenever a client feels stuck or considers promotion, based on the MBTI preference test, Jungian Coaching can offer an adventurous process of creativity, growth, and prosperity to empower the coachee's inferior function.

Epilogue

How Jungian psychology settled in Israel and into my Jungian Coaching practice. A personal glance

Back in 1985 I was referred to Mrs. Ella Amitzur, a Jungian analyst in Tel Aviv, to start Jungian analysis. It was the custom at that time to send the candidate for a chirology test as a preliminary requirement for starting the analytic therapy. I found myself, a young psychologist, climbing the old stairs of 1 Hayarkon St. Tel-Aviv to meet an old thin lady, with short white hair, moving energetically toward a room full of old German books, miniatures, sculptures, etchings, and modest wooden furniture, in an all-European-style apartment, much different from the interiors I was familiar with in our bourgeoisie suburb apartments of the city. Quite efficiently the lady, Julia Neumann, widow of the great Erich Neumann, asked me to cross my hands, smeared black ink on the palm of my left hand where apparently my left thumb happened to be positioned above my right hand's palm, stuck silk thin paper over my hand, and stained the lines of my hand. She rushed me to the toilet to wash my hands and returned to sit, record, and listen to my personality diagnosis. Much emphasis had been given to my connectedness to my unconsciousness, which was apparently a prerequisite to be accepted to Jungian analysis. In the well-respected Israeli newspaper *Haaretz* (October 4, 2011), Aviva Lori (died 2013) wrote "The Divine Neumanns" in honor of Erich Neumann's 100-year anniversary where she interviewed at length Dr. M. Neumann (psychoanalyst) and R. Leventhal–Neumann (psychologist and chirolist), both children of Julia and Erich Neumann. In the article, she writes that Neumann was born in Berlin in 1905 and passed away from cancer in Tel Aviv in 1960. Erich met Julia when he was 16 and gave her a book of Martin Buber with a dedication reading "our roads will meet again". We know they got married in 1928. In Berlin before the war, Neumann studied medicine and Julia studied special education. She gave birth to Micha in 1932 and in 1933 immigrated with her son to Palestine because she was Zionist but even more because of the antisemitic violence that prevailed in Germany at the upraise of the Nazi regime. Meanwhile Erich Neumann qualified himself as a Jungian Analyst with Jung in Zurich for an intensive year. He was 28 when he met with Jung who was 58 years of age. By summer 1933, Neumann joined his family in Tel Aviv. Previously to immigrating, Julia herself was qualified to

DOI: 10.4324/9780429351518-31

become Jungian analyst both by the "women of Jung" Emma Jung and Toni Wolff, and she also was qualified to become a chirologist by the well-known Julius Speer (a psycho-chirologist or hand reader in Berlin who was encouraged by Jung to develop this diagnostic method). Developing Depth Psychology in Israel (a newborn Levantine socialistic country absorbing immigrants, Holocaust survivors, and Jews from the Arab diaspora), Erich Neumann found it very challenging to assimilate in the country. He was very concerned by the country's ethical and cultural development and corresponded intensively with Jung about those issues. The Second World War disconnected him from his master and his intellectual father and partner, yet not surprisingly gave birth to immense creative productions. Between 1934 and 1947, Neumann did not meet Jung. After the Second World War they collaborated, and Neumann benefited from systematic support from Jung. Neumann published eleven books, and tens of articles. For the Israeli Jungian community, psychologists, and scholars, his base in Tel Aviv was a fountain of knowledge, inspiration, and solid school for Analytic psychologists.

Out of the second generation of Jungian Analysts in Israel, who were trained by Neumann, I was fortunate to acquire both therapy and supervision for many years by the late Ella Amitzur (1924–2009), Deborah Kucinski, and later on by Ily Weistub, Shulamit Stern, and my recent mentor Ruth Netzer (author of four important massive books and many analytic articles, unfortunately all written in Hebrew). I graduated from the three-year Jerusalem Jungian Seminars Program managed by Dr. Avi Baumann, Dr. Ily Weistub, Dr. Henry Abramowitz, and others. For years I practiced the Jungian approach in my Expressive Arts therapies and in my clinical work. Parallel I taught in the Academic College for Management in Tel Aviv, where I led a Master's practicum seminar under the title "Symbols and Archetypes in Organizations". In that seminar I applied Jungian Psychology to corporate life, tutoring my students to intervene with Jungian Coaching tools that I had gradually developed. This brought me to the notion to turn Jungian Psychology into a Jungian Coaching method.

Chapter 32

When the Shadow archetype met Lady Corona, a comprehensive case study about Jungian Coaching in Covid-19 pandemic era

During this time of the terrifying Corona pandemic that is paralyzing our lives, I wish to present a Jungian Coaching integrative approach to comprehend the challenges we face both on personal and professional levels. For now, let us just agree that Shadow in Jungian psychology refers to a person, a nation, or humanity's inferiority or malice (chapter 21). In this chapter I shall attempt to shed light on the dilemma of how external collective unconscious evil (in the sense that it is an invisible killer) evokes the collective and individual Shadows. Simply, how external autonomous negative and destructive power impacts the people and the world. I am interested in the manifested derivatives of the collective and the individual Shadows. When the Shadow archetype encounters Lady Corona, the complex of unconscious archetypes assemble, and it resembles the wedding feast between Zeus and Hera: "all who were summoned to the double wedding accepted with excited pleasure … to add zest to an already frenziedly anticipated occasion, Zeus issued a challenge: whoever could devise the best and most original wedding dish could ask any favor of him" (Fry, 2018, p. 75). Taking active part in this dreadful feast are the Persona archetype (daily habits), which opposes immediate spontaneous innovative and flexible adaptation; the Trickster archetype and how it intervenes into the picture; the negative side of Femininity (Anima) and how it flourishes on both sides – the virus and its victims; and the Masculine (Animus) principle and how vulnerable it becomes in such cases. In my opinion, the question relating to the desired remedy and cure is hidden in the secret of Melissa the bee, a shy little creature who offered Zeus magic honey for which she won the contest, but not without pain. (However, this belongs to the end of this chapter.)

Jung related to apocalyptic events as a result of nightmares he remembered during the period of his departure from Freud in 1913. In 'After the Catastrophe' (1945), he related to evil aspects caused by the human collective after the Second World War. John Goldhammer (2013), in "The End of Civilization; Did Jung Underestimate the Significance of His Own Dream", analyzed Jung's article. As we characterize the actual threat we face today, I wonder how irrelevant those thoughts are, because within the

DOI: 10.4324/9780429351518-32

Corona phenomena is an evil magic, which is invisible, trickily effective, disguised and occurs in different forms of its species, leaving us with the enigma of how it spreads so quickly and vastly throughout the world. I hope Corona is not directly caused or deliberately planned by human initiatives. However, the "Ego" (our conscious daily activities) relates to the "Shadow" as the Light to Shadow, says Jung, for the bigger the light (person's activities) the bigger the shadowy pitfalls. This statement brings to my mind the option that Humanity's light had begun to glimmer too strongly, to the extent that it blinded us, the creators of the enlightenment. Corona has violently diminished our Ego Activities and compelled us inwards.

Stein and Henderson (2020), in their article on Corona, speak of the inevitable "Transformation" into "Introversion", which will direct people from objects (aims) toward subjects (clients). Humanity stands up facing a different Shadow; not a Hiroshima's world war disaster (planned and created by the human brain), but rather a "Lady Corona"; the Coronavirus disease (COVID-19) where its mystery, arithmetic progression qualities, and impersonation produce fear, terror, and death, and a spontaneous eclipse. What happens psychologically in such a case, from a Jungian Psychology point of view, and how can a Jungian coach approach such a challenge in coaching settings?

The "Corona" obliges us to consider Shadow aspects of which we haven't previously been aware of, not only on the personal level but rather on the collective level: the sin of collective arrogance, hubris, and humanity's Ego inflation. Our generation witnessed the conquer of the moon, turned the Globus into a small village, increased low-cost travel, deciphered the human DNA, and turned artificial intelligence into practical daily practice. Our society arrogantly mocked the world's ecology and placed economic interests above hygiene, and our children adopted English as an international language and avoided learning our neighbors' languages. They blindly follow the global corporations' plot of consumption and "data culture". Unfortunately, all these made us face the life threats phenomena these days that can be explained in Jungian terms by the principles of "Compensatory-Function", the "Flipping Principle", and the rule that "Nothing is Sustainable".

In the span of one month, Humanity experienced an upheaval. In relating to balancing and compensatory function (chapters 6 and 7), Samuels (1985) states clearly that:

> By taking archetypal theory as a whole, we can see three types of sense-making link: polarity - the positive and negative, or personal and collective, or instinctual and spiritual, spectra of the archetype; complementary – the relative balance noticeable in psyche; interaction – the interplay of planes of imagery.

This means that we must accept that reality is also connected to the reverse – anti-reality. We witnessed G.H. Hagel's statement that everything becomes real only when encountered with its opposite, meaning the Corona threat teaches us the value of our lives. We must accept the parallel bass musical tone that lies under the melody of our realm. Corona is turning our lives upside down. The Jungian Dialectic Principle and the Unity of Poles in the coaching practice relates to the client's ability to accept contradicting ideas, which should not necessarily be threatening but rather open up options for creative collaborations, integration, and synthesis. In the Corona era this means that we must accept contradicting conditions and values as challenges, and we must accept and adopt these new realities and learn to act accordingly. I recently experienced inflexible colleagues and clients, as well as restricted learning communities, held back by a paranoid approach. They refused to listen to my call to "think outside of the box" and adopt business solutions which seem fitting during this long, unexpected, and unpredictable crisis. "Go to work" turns into "employ yourself at home", and "send the children to school" turns into "create a Sebastian Bach home conservatory". Real learning environments must be given up for the sake of long-distance virtual curiosity. This connects with the Jungian principle of Balancing and Compensatory Function. Those principles occur in coaching processes when the client considers inferior situations, non-attractive options, and limited potentials as developmental benefiting challenges. Whatever you lack you might strive to fill up, and what you over possess, you will mistakenly lose, claimed Jung, and Corona echoes it today. In Jungian Coaching the compensatory function principle is extremely valuable and prevails in most coaching interventions. This means that the compensatory function intends to balance the client's inclination by reducing or accelerating the expected. For example, if the client presents a dilemma, is asked by the coach to choose an image, and then comes up with a symbol or archetypal image that will represent the dilemma, the chosen image may function as a compensatory symbol. Stein and Henderson (2020) point out the dream, the prayer, and the work with symbolic images as contemporary requirements to lead clients in how to explore the knowledge of their inner world. In the Corona era, reality has turned into the irrational, unconscious quality realm, and powerful people, hectic executives, prosperous leaders, masters of control, and charismatic tricksters have turned abruptly into silhouettes who need to redefine themselves and justify new modes of adaptations. Yes, indeed, the Jungian Coach too must reshuffle his or her cards. My immediate family is spread out all over, and family gatherings have become a rare event. Yet last Friday, out of despair, I suggested a family Zoom meeting to welcome the Shabbat. I made an improvised decorated box and arranged a puppet show for my two-year-old granddaughter. I used vegetables and fruits instead of puppets. That interactive family event was much more heartwarming and significant than previous family meetings. Yes, we have now turned into subordinates of the kingdom of creativity.

Next is the Jungian principle of Materialism as it Relates to Spirituality. This theme will unfortunately prevail nowadays in most coach–client dialogues. When the client or corporation are terribly preoccupied by over-materialistic or financial problems, ethical or moral issues will burst out and require "spiritual balancing".

Those Jungian principles represent a sequence between polarities. The client, in presenting his dilemma, will locate himself pre consciously somewhere on the sequence between those extremes. It is the coach's major assignment not only to facilitate shifting actual experiences and acts along those poles but also to discover the benefits and drawbacks arising by acquiring the life and professional experiences that those sequences offer. Eventually and inevitably we shall now have to change values, behaviors, and approaches as a function of the client's flexibility to position himself/herself along those dual poles. However, it is crucial to understand that this "poled structure" is the normal psychic anatomy of our psyche.

Connecting and validating those terms is the "Flipping Principle" (chapter 7) based on Jung's Rosarium. The collaboration with Wolfgang Pauli crystalized Jung's understanding of the "Reversal Principle" and its reciprocity, namely, that the unconscious complements consciousness and there is always an "opposing material" standing in compensatory relationship to the "presented actual material". Keep in mind how the Corona pandemic forces human habits, values, and requirements to turn upside down and behave "with our heads in the ground and legs in the air". As a Jungian coach, once you adopt this way of thinking, manifested in the reverse principle of the overt and hidden, the Flipping Principle, you can effectively interpret overt and hidden relationships between "old habits" and new challenges, between old values and contemporary challenging situations and between despair and hope. This "Flipping Principle" adds profoundness and complexity to the understanding of nature in general and particularly to human relationships these days. In short what seems as a dead end, desperation, loss, chaos, fearful, impossible, unprofessional, and unethical can be served as potentials for change, growth, innovation, and magic.

Netzer (2004) dedicates her book to the Alchemy of the Soul and the Alchemy Process. When she specifies the stages of the alchemy process, she demonstrates the amazing parallel between metal versus mental processes (p. 173). Those descriptions of change processors are relevant to Jungian Coaching during times of crisis. In the Corona era, I urge the reader to consider applying the following alchemical techniques in our coaching sessions online. Often the coach and coachee avoid the direct change approach because it does not come without suffering (Goren-Bar, 2018, pp. 16–22). R. Netzer (2004) describes seven alchemical processes to obtain substantial change (chapter 16), yet in this chapter I will only present four practical and relevant ones to our time. The first technique is Solutio, which refers to melting the solid with water. In Jungians terms this means melting the conscious mechanisms into unconsciousness and emotions. When the coachee is too cognitive, when they rationalize and deny the difficult reality they are facing, when they think too much while the adequate response requires relating to their emotions, sentiments, and the consideration of irrational data in the equation, we need to consider involving the Solutio principle. (Example: a client in a Zoom session seems stubborn and persistent in insisting on having her clients come to her office to continue their coaching processes these days. When I ask her to explain to me her arguments, she rationalizes that we must stick to routine. I guess she hides her feelings behind those rationalizations. I simply ask how she feels these days and she bursts in a loud cry. She continuously sobs and shares with me her terror that she might lose what she achieved after long years of efforts. Now that she switched from cognitive into emotional, she can reevaluate her approach towards her work.) In the Hero Quest (chapter 25) we may find the "Crossing the Threshold" stage as an efficient experience for taking under consideration the emotional aspect of the dilemma alongside the cognitive decision making. In addition, connecting to the Feminine Principle is also advisable (which is discussed later in this chapter).

The second technique to consider these days is Kagulatio, meaning drying. This involves drying out the material from the emotional water and turning the liquid material into substantial, grounding, practical consideration. This is antithetical to the previous approach. If the coachee is hysterical, in panic, too emotional, too ambitious, too involved, or too enthusiastic, it is advisable to adopt the Kagulatio approach, meaning to learn to set aside the emotional stuff and act rationally. Holding on to the Masculine Principle is advisable. On the Hero Quest this experience will correspond to the "Atonement with the Father" stage. (Example: an executive in his thirties who initiated a start-up and invested all his savings in it suffers anxiety attacks and insomnia. His business requires open sky flights, which are restricted these days, so his new business seems lost. He is referred to coaching supported by his wife. In the coaching session he cannot stop talking, repeating hysterically how unlucky and destroyed he is. My impression is that he is drawn into his emotional turmoil. I ask him to take a paper and write down a list of immediate acts he must consider in his business. Surprisingly, in facing a concrete task he pulls himself together and collaborates with me.)

The third stage is Sublimation, meaning vaporization, transforming the impulsive concrete behavior or response into the spiritual and symbolic. I assume that soon we shall inevitably experience unfortunate losses, both of lives and fortune. When the client loses materialistic achievements and has no spiritual tools to balance his life experience, he might fall into moods, depression, addictions, or suicide attempts. Such states are represented on the Hero Quest at the stages of "The Woman as Temptress" and "Crossing of the Return Threshold". Sublimation connects to the principle of Materialistic vs. Spirituality. (Example: Now that corporate and business life is halted and people inevitably have free time, they should be helped to expose themselves to spiritual practices which can later on, after the crisis, be balanced with returning to routine tasks.)

Last, and regrettably very relevant, is the consideration of the alchemical principle Mortification, Death. Every move from one stage into another in life, any transformation or change, inevitably kills its previous existing presence, turning the present into the past with possible death experiences (metaphoric or actual). So, it is Negrado that deals with darkness, rot, decomposition, suffering and inventible torture. (Example: in realizing the inevitable economic destruction after the Corona decreases, as coaches, we shall have to help people rehabilitate their professional activities.) The loss and termination of professional and business initiatives will be associated with Death. "My business is gone, finished, my bank account is empty, my energies are somewhere else, I lost faith" – these statements call for a Mortification challenging coaching approach: express your loss, on the one hand, and see where there is a sprout of hope on the other. The Corona effect is disastrous on both life and economic prospects. People might lose life investments as well as people they care about deeply. Coachees involved with business, relationships, studies, as well as life events that arrive to an end must acquire an ability to let go of the past and enable new changes to take over. This is where Mortification needs to be applied and accepted.

Netzer (2020) on her online site brought up recently a whole gallery of Jungian concepts, archetypes, symbols, and mythos which correspond with the Coronavirus. Among them she mentioned the global dark side of the Shadow, the biblical mythos of the Ten Beatings of Egypt, Oedipus in search of the reason why a plague fell on his city, the Chaos versus the archetype of Wisdom and Knowledge, the archetypes of Death and Resurrection, the Hubris archetype, the archetype of the Decent opposing the Evil, the archetype of Unconsciousness, the Divined invisible, the archetype of the Horrible Great Mother, the archetype of Time and Temporality, the archetype of Diminishing, the Hero fighting the Monster, the mythos on the search for magic medicine, the Self and Meaning, the Belief and the Mythos of the Flood.

I chose to concentrate on three crucial archetypes and explain how they manifest in this current crisis. The interaction between those archetypes causes a "Corona complex". (Complex is an unconscious psychic "mixture of archetypes" that cause people to respond very strongly emotionally.) Presenting the archetypal effects all together during the Corona pandemic might cause the reader uneasiness. My approach corresponds with Dan Carlin's Hardcore History Podcast (2020); however, eventually I shall bring forth potential paradoxical benefits that one can draw out of this present devastating state.

"The Feast": Jungian Coaching with the Shadow, Persona and Anima archetypes in the Corona pandemic.

The Shadow in Corona crisis

Stein and Henderson (2020) speak about "Anima Mundi" (Jung's concept of global maternal libidinal love) and how Corona pandemic turned the world into "Umbra Mundi" – a world's Shadow. My clinical career brought me to the conclusion that there are three sorts of Shadows (Goren-Bar, 2018, chap. 4): Human Evil, Inferiority, and the White Shadow. Jungian Coaching focuses mostly on the last two (chapter 21). The Corona pandemic is shedding a collective Shadow on our modern Western lifestyle approaches: extensive consumption, exploitation, harassment, rush, short time process investments, over-regulations and procedures, crowdedness, loneliness, xenophobia, and racism seem to have been prominent features in our lives. Practical Jungian Coaching hardly relates to the global social collective Shadow but rather to individual and corporate Shadows. In the Corona case, the Shadow operates on all three levels: it penetrates the collective, the corporations, and the individuals. When the threat or challenge does not derive from the personal Shadow but rather from a forced major source, and where neither the coach nor the coachee is immune, it will take a while until clients will reach out for online coaching support and the coaching dialogue, then, will probably touch psycho-social-philosophical issues as well.

It is never too late to face and cope with one's own Shadow. It requires an optimistic, humanistic, and courageous approach. Dealing with the Shadow will keep the client humble, inevitably creative and knowledgeable. This is one of the most important insights Coronavirus teaches us. In situations where we are totally disoriented, paralyzed, ignorant, and helpless, it is expected to be able to halt, observe, breath in, stay still, and concentrate. This behavior is opposite to popular heroic instinctual immediate responses that were praised before the Corona era. The Jungian Coaching challenge nowadays is then to help the client dwell in "the belly of the whale" (the fifth stage in the Hero Quest). Baumann (2005) surveys the Shadow as an internal threat; however, in our case, we are interested in how clients deal with internal fears caused and stimulated by an external colossal collective threatening reality. In Corona time, not to act impulsively may turn into the very right response, and staying passive calls eventually for introverted introspections which in return may lift up unconscious contents, first the inevitable fears, and paranoia but later on creativity and out-of-the-box solutions. Habits and behaviors that before the Corona era were considered OCD (obsessive-compulsive disorder) phenomena have become routine regulations that are imposed on all human beings. The Shadow finally is acknowledged.

In principle, Jungian Coaching deals mostly with Shadow issues because people are finally seeking out coaching not because of its proven success, but due to their failures, underprivileged conditions, and concerns. Corona increased those challenges and hit even the strongest successful people. In this epoch of Corona, people are challenged to acquire new habits: in quarantine, families are squeezed together in small spaces, intimacy decreases, we increase our addictions to food, smoking, cellular calls, and social media. We are challenged by boredom as well as by aggression that bursts out, we are troubled by economic issues, we neglect basic requirements (health, physical, intellectuals, and socials), and we live under uncertainty and an obscure future. This sort of collective Shadow causes false and fake news, rumors, and hysterical responses such as mass consumption of food and paranoia. These are ideal terms for Shadow symptoms to emerge as the Ego is distressed. I expect severe outbursts of despair that will soon be reported by our clients. Coaching practice very likely will focus on reorganizing the Ego functioning of our client, supporting spiritual activities and helping clients to step out from their paralyzing comfort zone.

As an archetype, the Shadow has two sides: the negative (which we specified here), and the positive, the White Shadow. There are certain inevitable moments, events, or acts in a human's life, and specifically in the Corona era, when immoral acts are done for the sake of moral motives. Any voluntary acts of risk taking, such as helping people in need who were infected by the virus, are examples of the "White Shadow". If there will be shortages of food, we will unfortunately see reports of robbery. Promoted employees are fired these days, and human relationships swing between altruistic acts and human brutalities. In Jungian Coaching, the challenging issue with the White Shadow forces the coach and coachee into ethical dilemmas. We face a need to renovate the "old" coaching contract into an updated contract that suits online coaching. As with all contents that invade our mind, in the beginning the Shadow appears in a projective way: we are not aware of this negative trait in our personality that we deal with. Paradoxically, now squeezed in the quarantine we identify that negative trait in our significant others: mother, husband, business partner, best friend, a member of a team, a colleague, and our competitive partner or company. When we are aware of its prevalence in our personality, we sense anxiety and doubts.

The Persona in Corona time

"The Persona and Shadow archetypes are complementary structures", claims Stein (1998), "and exist in every developed human psyche" (p. 86). First to be crushed by the Corona pandemic was the Persona archetype. People found themselves working at home in their pajamas and workaholics whose working environment was their substitute home became "homeless". Teachers who stood in front of classes were pushed to become "technical background Zoom hosts". Businessmen, shop owners, restaurants, and employees lost their jobs. A job is not only an income but rather a spine of identity and that identity has suddenly faded away. Routines and regulations (which are the genes of the Persona) fell into pieces under the quarantine and isolation rules. Persona also touches the corporation's bond with the "outer world"; customers, providers, competitors, collaborators, and associates. They suddenly vanished, and there are increases in dismissals of employees and new modes of collaborations. Persona has to do with fashion, personal taste, marketing, branding, advertisement, the executive's symbols of status, the design of the office (open space vs. closed secretary battalion indoor office), personal card, proclaimed statement of belief, the corporate uniform, personal items, gadgets, icons, your bag, your car, your travel agent, your personal assistant, your friends, your club, and so many more – all were frozen, halted, postponed, or turned irrelevant. On the other hand, through the compensatory function, people started consuming intensively through the online hubs, companies such as Amazon, Wolt and others took the advantage and got swollen, The computer world flourished and human services are substituted by online long distance answering machines. The consequences of the Persona deterioration as a result of the Corona pandemic will be cleared only in the years to come. Obviously, millions are invested on the Persona level and millions will be lost. What is the Jungian coach's role now in redefining the Persona?

We know that a "functioning Persona" assures normal behavior and a "broken Persona" can predict psychosis. This means that if the Ego activities are significantly restricted, then, in Jungian terms, the Ego shrinks, and the person will fall inevitably into the "Self" archetype. The Self, being an archetype, has two sides: the positive (inspiration, integration, and creativity) and the negative (destruction, psychosomatic diseases, or emotional collapse). As "the Persona is the person that we become as a result of acculturation, education, and adaptation to our physical and social environments" (Stein, 1998, 89), I would like to consider here a challenging aspect of the Persona archetype and its relevance to coaching in the Corona time. In my opinion, this recent issue of "Persona trauma" phenomena caused by the Corona quarantine is one of the greatest threats we shall face in the immediate coaching dialogues. I suggest a "gradual rehabilitating" coaching process where the coach and client try to redefine the client's updated potential. The client's assets and hidden qualities are needed to be reexamined in order to redefine a new Persona. Coaching will need to step by step develop substitute "roles" and new meanings for a new professional and personal identity. It obviously will start with redefining the coaching contract online. This comes with the inevitable challenge to convince the traumatized client that online coaching can indeed be efficient and worth the money.

When Jung (1982) presents his ideas about Femininity and the Anima, he first deliberately presents the Persona and argues its positive and negative aspects. How does this relate to coaching? Because the Persona grants us safeties often within fake security zones (habitual arrogance and illusion) and because the Persona is connected to social standards and society's norms, Jung warns the reader about the Persona, "enemy of change", which is awaiting "out there" as an obstacle for change. This is a very important argument: If indeed the Persona according to Jung is a potential obstacle for change, and if many Personas will be crushed because of the Corona pandemic, then it seems that one of the advantages of the Corona crisis is to enable people to redefine or readjust their roles and connect to their true selves with which they will "turn the lemons into lemonade". Jung's wisdom on this aspect is so very relevant nowadays. Here is an existential paradox: the Persona, on the one hand, provides us with social stability and gratifications but at the same time turns out paradoxically to be preventing the client from executing significant change, prohibiting the coachee from not only modifying his life but even thinking about possible modifications. This reciprocity between the Persona archetype and other "Archetypal-Change-Activators" (the Hero, the Animus, the Creator, and many more) is very crucial in comprehending the intrinsic challenge of the Jungian Coaching processes. Now let us consider how challenging this dilemma is becoming in the Corona era. How can men express their despair, anguish, and helplessness in face of the economic disaster when their Persona is crushed? How can women, in a time of survival, display a firm Animus, repress their emotions, and struggle to provide basic needs for their families? We have become vulnerable, skinless, undefined, and we must find out the basic components of our "new life" with which we shall weave a new Persona. The coaching profession must be able to contribute to this contemporary challenge. In the Jungian Executive Coaching practice with Persona one should first start with the Pizza analysis, meaning the clients' activities and connection with society and fundamental acts that were blocked. It seems essential for our potential clients these days, being that they are so reluctant to quarantine for months, to rebalance their practical activities (career, money) with spiritual, community, self-growth, and environment nurturing activities.

On the corporate level, I see huge challenges for companies to redefine their Persona and update their connection with customers according to the new reality. For example, "Palantir, the $20 billion-valued Palo Alto tech company backed by Facebook- founder Peter Theil, has already handled a 17.3 million contract with one of the leading health bodies leading the charge against COVID-19" (Pub. By Forbes). Obviously, Bio-Sciences Labs are competing in discovering a Corona vaccine. Meanwhile delivery workers, medical personnel, and the police are now on the front lines while luxuries, leisure activities, shopping, and teachers are substituted into online and long-distance agents.

The Anima/Feminine Archetype interfacing 'Lady Corona'

In that recent interview, Stein and Henderson (2020) speak about the need to surrender inward these days. Stein (1998) claimed: "Where there is anima/

us, we want to go, we want to be a part of it, we want to join it, if we are not too timid or afraid of adventure" (117). He also claimed that "the topic of defining Anima and Animus has become in many ways the most controversial, for it raises profound gender issues and suggests essential differences in the psychology of men and women" (104). I wish to put most emphasis on the Corona pandemic and how Anima is involved in this catastrophe. The Anima (men's unconscious Feminine side) and the Feminine Principle are parallel concepts correlating with the database of the Great Mother (Chapter 18). The Feminine Principle manifests itself through two polarities: On the positive side; a world of life, nature, fertility, growth, protection, intuition, containment, patience, circulation, period, emotions, matter (ground, earthy), nurturing, and symbolization. R. Netzer (2020), on her blog, describes our "Home" as the positive side of the Feminine Principle and claims that while quarantined it turns into a capture cell. In addition, Corona stimulates the negative side of the Feminine Principle: people live by instincts and bestial drives, they try to survive, some fall to hysteria, others are depressed (melancholy). In times of survival people tend to surrender to their instincts. They consume, calculate, and take decisions that are not rational. People tend to withdraw inward; countries close their borders. In this case the "Home" turns into "Prison". The "individual" well-being is not on top of a leader's decisions; leaders speak about the tribe's vaccine. People learn inevitably to live under uncertainty; they cannot predict the near future. Corporations are crushed and cannot exist without short-term clear business plans. This creates terrible threats on the economy and markets, and causes immediate dismissals and eventually poverty. Yet this is the first stage. After the regression we might face overt aggression, hidden aggression (suicide), hostility, jealousy, and decreases of collaborations and partnerships. Humanity is turned into darkness; under the light of the moon, we shall need to lean on intuition, on instincts, and on irrational decisions. The Coronavirus behaves in accordance with the negative side of the Feminine archetype. In this its name "Corona" follows the circle crown, a Feminine sign. It is invisible, it disguises and spreads anonymously, it penetrates the body quietly and explodes fast and, symbolically, it finally attacks the breathing system and the heart, which leave the person totally helpless. Even more, it tends to liquidate the elderly, meaning it exterminates the weak and vulnerable, as is the indeed the basic rule in nature rules of survival.

However, as mentioned before, there is a positive side as well to the Feminine archetype. As our Ego activities narrow significantly we tend to circulate in a smaller way. This repetition, processing, patience, and gradual development characterized the positive side of Femininity. While locked in our homes, we paradoxically embrace these days. Another important principle is Unconsciousness - which is the domain of the Feminine Principle. In Corona days we need to surrender to our unconsciousness by meditating, walking in nature, cooking, and talking with people, creating art, and letting our irrational needs flow and fill our routine with surprises. We can transform ourselves with the help of a coach (such is the "Atonement with the Father" stage on the Hero Quest).

The Masculine-Father Principle opposes and compensates the Feminine Principle. Here lies the conflict we witness nowadays with medical teams, doctors, and nurses striving to save the struggling victims who gather and fill up the hospitals and the emergency health centers. These saviors represent the opposite of the negative Femininity. They present the Heroes and Heroines of our time, the positive aspect of the Patriarch. Death, under the Patriarch, is conceived as eradication of the individual and its consciousness. Life is conceived as a superior value. Love is individual and relatedness stands beyond emotional collectivity. Individuality is undividable, one entity and personal, and selfhood is praised. When the British government decided to adopt the "Tribe Vaccine" approach they voted for the Negative aspect of the Feminine Principle; however when Prince Charles or Prime Minister Boris Johnson got infected, suddenly the approach reversed to the positive side of the Masculine principle (chapter 190. In the Corona crisis, while governments calculate, plan, adjust, and try to run the health and economic systems, trying to avoid individual catastrophes by granting financial and health solutions, it sticks to the Masculine principle. Most biological scientists work day and night to find the remedy, vaccines, and equipment to fight the disease. If we summarized the main features that characterize the Masculine principle, we would count the linear line, speed, penetration-intrusion, rationale, mind, intellect, discipline, order, language, and individuality. However, if we analyze the efficiency of those traits in the midst of Corona time we unfortunately find out that the tests and quarantine (order, registration, follow-up) may partially sustain the threat, yet they lean back on Feminine principle solutions as well, such as "accumulated time", season of the year, and "tribe vaccines".

We will unfortunately witness these days an increase of "Tricksterism" behaviors both as a defensive response to life challenges and as a coalition between the Trickster and Shadow archetypes. Innocent, isolated, and troubled individuals might be tempted to pirate online initiatives using the desperate and offer miraculous economic initiatives. Some combination of Trickster/Shadow will be seen in partnerships, coalitions, and political life. The nation's desperation can end up with war.

Summary

By presenting the complexity of the Shadow, Persona, and the negative side of the Feminine Principle archetypes we can obtain new perspectives on the crisis of the Corona pandemic and how it affects the human psyche and people's behavior who suffer a severe blow. At times, this chapter describes a disaster; at other times it points out toward new horizons, inevitable challenges, and a need for innovative approaches toward business, communications, life well-being, and coaching.

Toward ending, let us return to Stephen Fry's (2018) *Greek Myths Retold*. By telling the myth of the wedding of Zeus and Hera, he introduces Melissa, the bee (Meli in Greek = honey). Her "amphora filled almost to the top with a sticky, amber-colored goo" entitled her to win the food competition of the feast. This story offers a coaching approach to the Corona pandemic. As a reward to her successful dish Melissa asked: "Give me, great Zeus, such a weapon, a fatal one, that will kill any who dare to steal my precious stock of honey". Zeus furiously shouted: "This silly, flighty dot of a creature was demanding a mortal sting, was she?" and punished her: "While it will bring a sharp pain to the one you sting, it is you and to your kind that it will bring death" (79). Here the ancient Greeks teach us what seems essential nowadays in this Corona pandemic era: a new coaching approach combining creativity and innovative challenges (honey) with a new mode of communication with Zoom collaborations, an adaptation of the "Reduction Principle", and respect for basic human lives, reciprocity, trust, and modesty.

Bibliography

Bala, M. (2010). The clown: An archetypal self-journey. *Jung Journal: Culture and Psyche, 4*(1), 50–71.

Baumann, A. (2005). *Grimm fairytales as a mirror of the soul's dark side: Grimm fairytales as a mirror of the soul's dark side.* Israel: Modan Pub. House.

Bolen, J. S. (1989). *Gods in everyman,* Hebrew translation. Israel: Modan Pub. House.

Bradley Zimmer, M. (1983). *The mists of Avalon.* New York: Alfred A. Knopf Pub.

Bridges, W. (2010). *Character of organizations: Using personality type in organization development.* London: Nicholas Brealey Pub.

Campbell, J. (1988). *The hero with a thousand faces.* London: Paladin.

Carlin, D. (2020). *Podcast.* Retrieved from https://www.ynet.co.il/articles/0,7340,L-5 713845,00.html

Castillejo, I. C. (1973). *Knowing woman: A feminine psychology,* Hebrew translation. Tel-Aviv: Modan Pub. House.

Colman, A. (1992). Depth consultation. In S. Murray & J. Hollwitz (Eds.), *Psyche at work: Workplace applications of Jungian analytical psychology.* Wilmette, IL: Chiron Publications.

Corlett, J. & Pearson, C. (2003). *Mapping the organizational dynamics and change.* Florida: Center of Applications of Psychological Type, Inc.

Denise, L. (1997). The feminine in the foundations of organizational psychology. *The Journal of Applied Behavioral Science, 33*(1), 7.

Edinger, E. (1984). *The creation of consciousness.* Toronto: inner City Books.

Fry, S. (2018).*Mythos: The greek myths retold.* London: Penguin Random House.

Furth, G. (1988). *The secret world of drawings: Healing through art.* Boston, MA: Sigo Press.

Gimbutas, M. & M. R. Dexter (2001). *The living goddesses.* London: University of California Press.

Goldberg, R. (2001). The consultant as hero. *Organization Development Journal, 19,* 3.

Goren-Bar, A. (2018). *The secrets of expressive arts therapy and coaching: A dialogue between master and disciple* (Vol 1 & 2). Createspace.

Goren-Bar, A. (2019). *Clinical expressive arts therapy in therapy and practice: Psychodynamic snapshots.* Newcastle upon Tyne: Cambridge Scholars Publishing.

Greenfield, B. (1983). The archetypal masculine: It's manifestation in myth and its significance for women. *Journal of Analytical Psychology*, 28, 33–35.

Grifin, D. (1989). *Archetypal process, self and divine in Whitehead, Jung and Hillman*, Evanston, IL: Northwestern University Press.

Groesbeck, C. (1975). The archetypal image of the wounded healer. *Journal of Analytical Psychology*, *20*(2), 122–145.

Guggenbuhl-Craig, A. (1971). *Power in the helping professions*. New York: Spring.

Guirard, F. (1968). *New Larousse encyclopedia of mythology*. England: The Hamlyn Publishing Group Limited.

Harari, Y. N. (2013). *Sapiens: A brief history of mankind*, Hebrew Language Copyright, Kinneret, Zmora-Bitan. Israel: Dvir – Pub. House.

Harari, Y. N. (2018). *21 lessons for the 21st. century*, Hebrew Language Copyright, Kinneret, Zmora-Bitan. Israel: Dvir – Pub. House.

Heukelom, F. (2011). *Three explanations for the Kahneman-Tversky Programme of the 1970s*. Taylor and Francis Online, 05 Apr 2011.

Hopcke, R. (2007).*Men's dreams, men's healing*, Hebrew translation. Tel Aviv: HaKibbutzim Publ.

Jacobi, J. (1964). Symbols in individual analysis. In *Man and his Symbols*. London: Picador, Published by Pan Books.

Jacoby, M. (1990).*Individuation and narcissism: The psychology of the Self in Jung and Kohut*. London: Routledge.

Jaffe, A. (1964). Symbolism and the visual arts. In *Man and his symbols*. London: Picador, Published by Pan Books.

Janis, I. L. (1982). *Groupthink: Psychological studies of policy decisions and fiascoes*. Amazon.

Jones, M. O. (1996). *Studying organizational symbolism*. Thousand Oaks, CA: Sage Publications.

Jung, C. G. (1954). The practice of psychotherapy. *The Collected Works*, 16

Jung, C. G. (1954). *The psychology of the transference*, from collected works, Bollingen Series (Vol 16). Princeton, N.J.: Princeton University Press.

Jung, C. G. (1954). *The structure and dynamics of the psyche. On the nature of the psyche*. The collected Works. Bollingen Series (Vol 8). Princeton, NJ: Princeton University Press.

Jung, E. (1957). *Animus and Anima*. Putnam, CT: Spring Publications.

Jung, C. G.(1963). Memories, dreams, reflections. In *Flamingo*. Fontana Paperbacks.

Jung, C. G. (1964). *Man and his symbols*. London: Picador.

Jung, C. G. (1967). *The Alchemical studies, from collected works, Bollingen Series, Vol. 13*. Princeton, NJ: Princeton University Press.

Jung, C. G. (1969). *Four archetypes: Mother, birth, Spirit, Trickster*. London: Ark Paperback.

Jung, C. G. (1976). *Aspects of the masculine*. Princeton, NJ: Princeton University Press.

Jung, C. G. (1976). *Alchemical studies*. Princeton, NJ: Princeton University Press.

Jung, C. G. (1976). *Psychological types*. Princeton, NJ: Princeton University Press.

Jung, C. G. (1976). *Aspects of the feminine*. Princeton, NJ: Princeton University Press.

Jung, C. G. (1982). *Aspects of the feminine, from the collected works of C.G. Jung.* Princeton, NJ: Princeton University Press.

Jung, C. G. (1983). *Memories, dreams, reflections.* London: Flamingo published by Fontana Paperbacks.

Jung, C. G. (1989). *Psychology and alchemy.* London: Routledge.

Jung, C. G. (1989). *Aspects of the masculine, from the collected works of C.G. Jung.* Princeton, NJ: Princeton University Press.

Jung C. G. (2009). The Red Book. In S. Shamdasani (Eds.), *Foundations of the Works of C.G. Jung.* New York: W. W. Norton. & Co in Philemon Series.

Kalsched, D. E. (2019). Opening the closed heart: Affect focused clinical work with the victims of early trauma (in his prominent plenary paper: for IAAP Congress Vienna).

Kast, V. (1992). *The dynamics of symbols.* New York: Fromm International Pub. Corporation.

Kast, V. (1993). *Imagination as space of freedom.* New York: Fromm International Pub. Corporation.

Ketola, T. (2012). Losing your Self: Managerial persona and shadow pressures killing responsible leadership. *Journal of Management Development, 31*(5), 470–487.

Kociatkiewicz, J. (2009). Experiencing the shadow: Organizational exclusion and denial within experience economy. *Organization, 17*(2), 257–282.

Matthews, R. (2002). Competition archetypes and creative imagination. *Journal of Organizational Change and Management, 15*, 461–476.

McCully, R. S.(1987). *Jung and Rorschach. A study in the archetype of perception.* Dallas, Texas: Spring Publications, Inc.

Meier, C. (1949). *Ancient incubation and modern psychotherapy.* Evanston, IL: Northwestern University Press, 1967.

Myers-Briggs Type Indicator instrument, MBTI, 3rd Edition (2009). Printing, CPP, U.S.A.

Nagel, C. (2020). *Psychodynamic coaching: Distinctive features.* London and New York: Routledge.

Netzer, R. (2004). *The quest for the self: Alchemy of the soul, symbols and mythology.* Israel: Modan Pub. House

Netzer, R. (2008). *The magician, the fool and the empress, tarot cards in the cycle of life and therapy.* Israel: Modan Pub. House

Netzer, R. (2011). *The hero quest.* Israel: Modan Pub. House.

Netzer, R. (2014). On the collective in the Jungian Individuation Process. In *Towards the self.* Reuben Mass Pub. (Translation from Hebrew)

Netzer, R. (2019). *The heroine's journey: The journey to the feminine self.* Israel: Modan Pub. House.

Netzer, R. (2020). Archetypes and mythos in corona era. https://www.hebpsy.net/blog_Post.asp?id=4675

Neumann, E. (1949). *The origin and history source of consciousness.* New York.: Bollingen Foundation, Inc.

Neumann, E. (1955). *The great mother.* New York: Bollingen Foundation, Inc.

Neumann, E. (1963). *Depth psychology and new moral.* Tel Aviv: Shoken Pub. House

Neumann, E. (1974). *Art and the creative unconscious.* New York: Bollinger, Princeton

Pearlman, J. (2016). *Australian foreign affairs and the world editor of The Saturday Paper*. Sydney, Australia.

Remington, N. (2007). The leadership archetype: A Jungian analysis of similarities between modern leadership theory and the Abraham myth in the Judaic-Christian tradition. *Journal of Business Ethics, 72*(1), 125–129.

Robbins, A. (1989). *The Psychoaesthetic experience: An approach to depth-oriented treatment*. New York: Human Science Press, Inc.

Samuels, A. (1985). *Jung and the Post-Jungians*. London and New York: Routledge.

Samuels, A. (1991). *A critical dictionary of Jungian analysis*. London and New York: Routledge

Schwartz-Salant, N. (1982). *Narcissism and character transformation*. Toronto, Canada: Inner City Books.

Sedgwick, D. (1994). *The wounded healer: Countertransference from a Jungian perspective*. London: Routledge

Smith, C. (2002). Leading change: Insights from Jungian interpretations of The Book of Job. *Journal of Organizational Change and Management, 15*(5), 448.

Starr-Glass, D. (2002). The voice of the shuttle, mythical and organizational transformation. *Journal of Organizational Change and Management, 15*, 5.

Stein, M. (1998). *Jung's map of the soul, an introduction*. Open court, Chicago: Carus Pub. Company.

Stein, M. & Henderson, R. (2020). A world shadow: Covid 19. Interview with M. Stein and Rev. Dr. R. Henderson. Retrieved from https://chironpublications.com/a-world-shadow-covid-19/

Stone, H. & Winkelman, S. (1985). *Embracing our selves: Voice dialogue manual*. California: Devours and Company, Publisher.

Tannen, R. S. (2007). *The female trickster, the mask that reveals. Post-Jungian and Postmodern psychological perspectives on women in contemporary culture*. East Sussex: Routledge

Toub, G. (2013). Jung and gender. In *Jung Page online educational resources for Jungian community*. Houston, TX: Jung Center of Houston.

Von Franz, M. L. (1964). The process of individuation. In *Man, and His Symbols*, Picador Pub. By Pan Books.

Von Franz, M. L. & Boa, F. (1988). *The way of the dream*. Toronto: Windrose Films LTD.

Weaver, R. (1964). *The old wise woman*. London: Vincent Stuart.

Whan, M. (1987). *Chiron's wound: Some reflections on the wounded healer*. In N. Schwartz-Salant& M. Stein (Eds.), *Archetypal Processes in Psychotherapy*. Wilmette, IL: Chiron Publications.

Zinkin, L. (1979). The Collective and the personal. *Journal of Analytical Psychology, 24*(3), 227–250.

Appendix

To become a Jungian coach, certified by the International Coaching Federation (ICF), please refer to Dr. Avi Goren-Bar at dravigb1@gmail.com and attend our Jungian Coaching School Online, which is an ACSTH-Approved Coaching Specific Training Hours program, at https://jungiancoachingschool.com.

Index

Milton Keynes UK
Ingram Content Group UK Ltd.
UKHW031532301124
451789UK00019B/398

9 780367 367992